WHAT'S THE POI

"A highly readable and provocative book, which both confronts and challenges us to seriously re-think current assumptions about educational practice. Claxton is one of the most important educational writers of our time."

Clarissa Williams, President of the National Association of Head Teachers

"That very rare thing, an up-to-the-minute and gripping read on what learning's all about. Invaluable for teachers and parents alike. This book will challenge all your assumptions about how we are educating children, and make you think urgently about the need for fundamental change. Guy Claxton is right at the cutting edge of his field."

Hilary Wilce, author of Help Your Child Succeed at School

"This book is a must-read for us all, not just those interested in formal education. In his brilliant unpacking of what it is to become a good learner, Guy shows us how to create environments that encourage people to learn, how to take risks, how to challenge, empathise, play, and innovate. This book should persuade politicians around the world that what future generations need most – to be both happy and productive – is the capacity to learn, and that schools can and must teach it."

Professor Kathy Sykes, University of Bristol, Television presenter,
Alternative Therapies, Rough Science, *and* Mind Games

"A hymn of praise to the qualities crucial to learning, as well as an informed and reliable guide to nurturing them."

Howard Gardner, Hobbs Professor of Cognition and Education,
Harvard Graduate School of Education

"Guy Claxton gets right to the heart of an issue that is one of the most important for shaping 21st century society."

Baroness Susan Greenfield, Director of the Royal Institution

"Education is failing our students disastrously and so are most education reforms. In this powerful, passionate, and persuasive book, Guy Claxton argues that the challenge is no longer to reform education but to transform it. The only way to do that is through a genuine revolution in how we think about learning – and about teaching. Guy Claxton says why – and he also says how."

Sir Ken Robinson, author of The Element: A New View of Human Capacity

"Comparing how well young minds *can* work with how poorly schools *do* work, Guy Claxton celebrates the curiosity, courage, and imagination of young learners and constructs a vision of education that would kindle rather than quench such virtues."

David Perkin

School of Education and
or of The Eureka Effect

ABOUT THE AUTHOR

Guy Claxton is one of the UK's foremost thinkers on creativity, learning, and the brain. He is Director of the Centre for Real-World Learning at the University of Winchester, and the author and editor of over twenty books on learning and creativity, including the best-selling *Hare Brain, Tortoise Mind: Why Intelligence Increases When You Think Less*.

GUY CLAXTON

WHAT'S THE POINT OF SCHOOL?

REDISCOVERING THE HEART OF EDUCATION

ONEWORLD

OXFORD

A Oneworld Paperback Original

Published by Oneworld Publications 2008
Reprinted 2009 (twice)

ISBN 978–1–85168–603–2

Typeset by Jayvee, Trivandrum, India
Cover design by Keenan Design
Printed and bound in Great Britain by Bell & Bain

Oneworld Publications
185 Banbury Road
Oxford OX2 7AR
England
www.oneworld-publications.com

Learn more about Oneworld. Join our mailing list to
find out about our latest titles and special offers at:

www.oneworld-publications.com

Contents

Preface

The only time my education was interrupted was while I was at
school.

Winston Churchill

The purpose of education is to prepare young people for the future.
Schools should be helping young people to develop the capacities they
will need to thrive. What they need, and want, is the confidence to talk
to strangers, to try things out, to handle tricky situations, to stand up
for themselves, to ask for help, to think new thoughts. That is not too
much to ask – it is every young person's basic educational entitlement.

But they are not getting it. There is no evidence that being able to
solve simultaneous equations, or discuss the plot of *Hamlet*, equips
young people to deal with life. We have lazily assumed that, somehow,
it must do, but research shows that even successful students are often
left timid and unsettled when they step outside the narrow comfort
zones of their academic success. We agonise about the content of the
syllabus, and the dumbing down of examinations, yet the core failure
of education to prepare young people for their complex and uncertain
futures passes, year after year, almost without comment.

This is shocking; and it is dangerous. Education has lost the plot,
and it urgently needs to recover its core purpose. Without the confidence that they are equal to the challenges they face, young people are
at risk. They are, as all the surveys show, prone to becoming anxious
and insecure, and to acting in the self-destructive ways that typify
people under stress. This is bad for them, bad for their families, bad for

their communities, bad for their employers, and bad for their countries. Politicians claim to put education at the heart of their concerns,
and they are right to do so. But they are wrong if they think that tinkering with the syllabus or the examination system will fix it. They
need the courage to go deeper.

This book provides a much-needed new perspective on schooling.
We are familiar with the perspective of *qualifications*: the concern to
monitor and measure how much of the curriculum has passed successfully into the mind of a student. And we are equally familiar with
the perspective of *content*: the concern with selecting and organising
the subject-matter of schooling. But we are much less familiar with
what I shall call the perspective of the *epistemic apprenticeship*: the idea
that school is a protracted training in particular ways of thinking,
learning and knowing (that's what 'epistemic' means: to do with the
ways people think, learn and know). Just as an apprentice jeweller or
mason carries out tasks that are designed to develop certain skills and
sensibilities, so we can look at education as a long-term training in certain kinds of thinking, remembering, writing, researching and com-
municating.

When Albert Einstein said that 'education is what remains after one
has forgotten everything one learned at school' it is those skills and
attitudes that he was referring to. If your schooling required you, lesson after lesson, to copy down facts, remember them accurately and
reproduce them when prompted, it was the skills of note-taking and
memorisation that you were practising, and the attitude of unques-
tioning acceptance that you were cultivating. If, on the other hand,
your curriculum was built around groups researching self-chosen
projects, then it was the skills of collaboration and discussion, and the
attitude of self-organisation, that were being inculcated. This perspective is not an alternative to the other two. To start paying attention to
the learning habits children are developing does not mean you no
longer care about the content, or about quality. The young jeweller or
mason needs specific stones to work with, and someone to judge how
well they are doing. But the point of the apprenticeship is not the
immediate performance so much as the cumulative development that
is going on behind the specific tasks. And if we are serious about

education being a preparation for the future, it is the quality of these learning skills and attitudes that matters in the long run.

The core confidence that young people need, and many of them lack, derives from a number of personal qualities – what, in this book, I will call their learning muscles. These are curiosity, courage, investigation, experimentation, imagination, reasoning, sociability and reflection. These are not just skills, although each has a skilful component. They are qualities of mind – pleasures and inclinations as much as abilities. When children have been helped to develop these learning muscles, they feel more confident, and are more willing to engage intelligently with the difficulties in their lives. These vital qualities are perfectly capable of being strengthened and cultivated by education – but in the pressure to push up literacy rates and exam passes, most schools have come to ignore and even subvert this most basic of their functions. All too often the quest for results serves to undermine the foundations of self-confidence rather than to strengthen them. Young people – some of them skilful exam-passers – become less curious as a result of their education, not more. They lose their capacity for wonder and critical questioning. Rather than becoming bolder and braver, they become more docile and fragile in the face of difficulty. They learn to think narrowly rather than broadly, to compete rather than cooperate, to be frightened of uncertainty and the risk of error that accompanies it. Education is in dereliction of its duty to the next generation if schools are not fostering these strengths in their students.

The disaffection with the methods and subjects of the traditional curriculum is an acute problem at the moment, but it is not a new one. The great American philosopher John Dewey wrote about it 70 years ago:

> How many students, for example, were rendered callous to ideas, and how many lost the impetus to learn because of the way in which learning was experienced by them? How many of them acquired special skills by means of automated drill so that their power of judgement and capacity to act intelligently in new situations was limited? How many came to associate the learning process with ennui and boredom? How many found what they did learn so foreign to the situations of life outside school as to give

them no power of control over the latter? How many came to
associate books with dull drudgery, so that they were 'condi-
tioned' to all but flashy reading matter?[1]

How many of today's school-leavers are still suffering the same kind of
mental abuse? We cannot – indeed must not – ignore the character-
forming nature of school. But the question is: what capacities and attitudes towards knowing and learning do we want to help today's young
people to cultivate. As a society, we can't afford to produce large numbers of young adults who see themselves as having failed at learning.
They cost us too dearly. Each year 150,000 school-leavers enter the
post-school world unable to count properly[2] – by any reckoning a failure of the system. As parents, we should not tolerate an institution that
both compounds our children's insecurity, rather than ameliorating it
and fails to teach so many of them basic skills.

In thrall to content and qualifications, we have forgotten the deeper
purpose of education. In the rush to make young people into successful exam-passers, we have overlooked their deeper need to become
successful *people*, eager to learn and grow in the real-life world of work,
leisure and relationships – and to become successful people they need
a rich set of useful, general-purpose habits of mind that will stand
them in good stead whatever they want or need to turn their hand to.
This book describes what an up-to-date, really useful epistemic
apprenticeship would look like, and how schools can provide it.

Building learning power

I first realised that school is, above all, a place where children go to
learn how to use their minds through my work as a cognitive scientist.
Since the publication of my first book in 1979, I have been fascinated
by the ways people learn – and how they can get better, and worse, at
learning. In 1984 I reviewed the research on learning in a book called
Live and Learn, and I updated that work in another book in 1990 called
Teaching to Learn. But it was not till a chance encounter with a primary
headteacher called Peter Mountstephen in 1997 that I began to work
directly with teachers and pupils, to explore how to put practical

flesh on the scholarly bones of my ideas. I was convinced that it was possible, in theory, to help young people become more powerful and effective learners. Working with Pete and the staff, governors, parents and pupils at his school enabled me to begin to devise the simple techniques that would translate psychological insight into educational reality.

My work in schools since that time led to the development of the practical programme that schools know as 'Building Learning Power', or BLP for short. Working with a small Bristol-based company, TLO Ltd, we devised ways to help schools to see what is possible, and to shift their habits in small but critical ways. We have carried out research projects in Cardiff, Bristol, Oxfordshire and elsewhere, to monitor and evaluate the effects. With colleagues at the University of Bristol, I have developed ways in which schools and pupils can keep track of their own developing 'learning fitness' and monitor their progress. Working in schools and meeting teaching professionals at conferences has enabled me to refine the programme and evaluate its success in classrooms both in the UK and internationally. Many of the ideas explored in this book have developed out of this exchange with schools.

Here is a small example of BLP in action. Julie Green's year five class are doing a lesson on magnets. A series of small experiments has been laid out around the room, and the children will go around in groups of three, carry out the experiments, and see what happens. But Miss Green explains to them that they will also be stretching their *questioning muscles*, because when they have made their observations, she wants them to think up the kinds of questions they think a scientist might be stimulated to ask. 'If the magnet does this, what would that make you wonder? What would you want to find out next?' she asks them. At the end of the lesson, the children share their observations and their questions – and then get involved in an animated discussion about 'What makes a good scientific question?' and 'How are scientists' questions special?'

These children are not only learning about magnets; they are, at the same time, sharpening their understanding of how different kinds of questions are good for different kinds of purposes. At the end of the lesson, Julie asks them to think of somewhere in their out-of-school lives where those kinds of questions would be helpful – and as they leave for their playtime, the children are happily discussing how they could use what they have learned in their swimming practice, or when they are watching a nature programme on television.

These children may not ever need to use what they have learned about magnets – but learning about good questioning will be useful for the rest of their lives. They are having their powers of curiosity stimulated and refined, and they are thinking about how useful that can be in real life. Compare this to a more familiar kind of lesson, in which the aim is merely to learn the correct answers, and in which the only questioning voice is that of the teacher. Researchers have found that, in normal classrooms, in both primary and secondary schools, children are hardly ever stimulated to ask their own questions, or to think about the nature of questioning. One study found that, in the space of a lesson, students volunteered just two questions to the teacher's eighty-four. Over a school year, young people asked an average of just one question a month.[3] What Julie Green has done is make a small, manageable shift to her classroom practice that, added to a dozen others like it, can make all the difference to her students' future confidence to think and wonder. You may think this just sounds like good teaching – but it is surprisingly rare.

Although many teachers are becoming familiar with the ideas and possibilities of 'learning to learn', these ideas have not yet seeped out, as fully as they need to, into the thinking of parents and the wider public. This book aims to rectify that. For I believe it is only when parents in their thousands truly realise what is at stake, and what is possible, that politicians will begin to respond with the speed and commitment that is required. As we will see, it is not yet more tinkering with the content and the exams that is needed. It is a whole-hearted exploration of questions such as these:

- What kind of curriculum is going to be best suited to developing the mentalities and identities that will enable young people to prosper?
- What kinds of activities, based on that knowledge, will stretch and develop those qualities most effectively?

- How can we ensure that what is developed will be disembedded from the context of school, so that it will give young people a genuine purchase on the problems and challenges of their real lives, both presently and in the future?
- How do we organise schools so everyone will feel that they are there to improve something useful, and are able to do so, and not that they are constantly being reminded how 'bright' or 'weak' they are?

To effect a thorough change we have to start by seeing just how bad things are. We have to understand what it is that young people really need, what schools are actually providing, and acknowledge the gulf between the two. And then we have to establish, beyond all possible doubt, that the kind of educational reform that has been going on for more than a hundred years is not going to work. We have to abandon the vain hope that such tinkerings are ever going to do the trick. Only once we have done that can we launch the main argument of the book: that a different kind of change is both necessary and possible. With a bit of imagination, and a modicum of courage, education can rediscover its heart and soul.

This book will take you into classrooms and living rooms, and show you the many affordable, ingenious ways in which young people's spirit of adventure can be developed. H. G. Wells said that human history becomes more and more a race between education and catastrophe. A little dramatic perhaps, but there is no doubt that rediscovering the true purpose of education is a matter of urgency. This is the territory where the debate needs to be happening. The authoritative Cambridge review of primary education in 2007 found that literacy levels have remained almost static since the 1950s – an unpalatable fact that ministers seem loath to accept. Over the same period, children's enjoyment of reading – their feel for its pleasures and purposes – has significantly declined: an appalling and unacceptable cost that the same ministers appear blithely to discount.[4] If politicians and policymakers are not going to do it, then parents and teachers will have to lead the debate about what should happen in our schools. It is my fervent hope that this book will help them do it.

Acknowledgements

Thanks are due to a good many people. There are the literally thousands of teachers, headteachers and advisers I have talked and worked with over the last ten years, who have helped me see how to turn the theory into practice. Iniquitously, I'll single out just a few: Rosemary Bailey, Beverley Ball, Tony Barnes, Danny Bullock, Martin Burt, Andy Carpenter, Janet Cassford, Liz Cooper, Leanne Day, Raegan Delaney, Kate Drew, Kay Edwards, Louise Edwards, Armando di Finizio, Chris Glass, Julie Green, Alice Griffith, Kevin Hogston, Maxine Houghton, Rachel Hutchinson, Sarah Jackson, Jess Jones, Stephen Jones, Reena Keeble, Liz Ladd, Jane Leo, Rachel MacFarlane, Kate Mason, Peter Mountstephen, Ros Pollard, Abi Price, Natasha Reeves, Karen Roofe, Vicki Scale-Constantinou, Jane Simister, Julian Swindale, Ray Tarleton and Michael Whitworth. My colleagues at TLO Ltd, Gillian Baxter, Maryl Chambers and Graham Powell, have played a major role in developing and disseminating the Building Learning Power framework. At the University of Bristol, Patricia Broadfoot and Ruth Deakin-Crick collaborated on the development of ways of assessing 'learning power'; Martin Hughes and Pam Greenhough helped me think about the relationship between school and home; Federica Olivero, Ros Sutherland and Martin White joined me in organising the two seminal *This Learning Life* conferences; and Sara Meadows helped me think about how young children learn their intelligence. In the wider world, my thinking has benefited greatly from continuing conversations with Chris Brookes, Margaret Carr, Bill Lucas and Chris Watkins. In preparing the book the wise counsel of Marsha Filion and her colleagues Kate Smith and Dawn Sackett at Oneworld has been invaluable. It is a better book because of them. And finally, heartfelt thanks to Jude for all her love, support and understanding.

1

Stress: the children's epidemic?

There is a crisis at the heart of our society . . . Children represent the
future of our country, and from the findings of this report they . . .
feel unsafe and insecure, have low aspirations and put themselves
at risk.

Sir Al Aynsley Green, Children's Commissioner for England

Before schools can genuinely begin to meet the needs of young
people we need to understand what those needs are. We must understand what their world is like, how they are coping, what the key
stresses are, what their futures hold and what tools and resources they
require to live successfully in the world beyond the school gates.
Gaining some clarity about these questions is what this chapter is
about.

Many young people live happy lives, and relish their schooldays.
They like their teachers, enjoy at least some of their subjects, are good
enough at the things school values to feel good about themselves, and
feel they have a reasonable chance of doing well enough in their exams
to get where they want to go. But many are not so fortunate. And while
many of those who are struggling come from poor and unstable families and communities, a good many of them come from homes that are
apparently stable and well-off. You may know, as I do, loving families
in which the parents feel that their teenaged child has 'gone off the
rails' or 'got in with a bad crowd'. Many young people run away from
home, get drunk or take drugs, get pregnant, fail their exams, develop

eating disorders or self-harm. These are clearly situations of degrees of seriousness – exams can be retaken for example while self-harm or drug addiction can require years of recovery – but the central issue is that we need to recognise that there are deep currents with which all young people, no matter what their family background, are having to cope.

Young people's mental health

The surveys and statistics show that, for more and more young people every year, fearfulness, self-doubt, self-consciousness and insecurity are constant themes. In 2004 the prestigious *Journal of Child Psychology and Psychiatry* reported the results of an extensive and rigorous study comparing teenagers' mental health in 1974, 1986 and 1999. The report begins:

> The mental health of teenagers has sharply declined in the last twenty-five years, and the chances that fifteen-year-olds will have behavioural problems such as lying, stealing and being disobedient have more than doubled. The rate of emotional problems such as anxiety and depression has increased by 70% in adolescents.

The researchers found that boys are more likely to exhibit behavioural problems, while girls are more likely to experience emotional problems – as many as one in five fifteen-year-old girls, in fact.[5]

A 2005 survey of their readers by girls' teen magazine *Bliss* corroborated this picture. Teenage girls feel stressed on all fronts – at home, at school and with friends. They feel under pressure to look good, act cool, behave responsibly and succeed academically. Nine out of ten have felt depressed, 42% 'feel low' regularly, and 6% think 'life is not worth living'. One in three fourteen-year-old girls say they drink alcohol every week. Two out of every three say they have been bullied. 37% say they 'suffer from obsessive compulsive disorder'(feeling bound to carry out a range of superstitious rituals or repetitive actions in order to ward off trouble or make themselves feel safe).[6] Another survey in 2006 found that teenage drinking has almost doubled in the last four years alone. More than a third of fifteen-year-old girls describe themselves as regular drinkers, and it is middle-class girls from traditional, so-called stable homes, who are drinking the most. Over half of all sixteen-year-olds have tried illegal drugs.[7]

In 2007 a Unicef report on the well-being of children and adolescents ranked the UK worst overall out of twenty-one wealthy nations on a range of indicators. British children are more likely to have got drunk or had sex than those of any other developed country. One of the indicators on which the UK was right at the bottom was peer relationships. Only 40% of British children over eleven described their peers as 'kind and helpful' compared, with over 80% in Switzerland. (Holland and Scandinavia came out top overall; the USA was next to last, only slightly better than the UK.)

Commenting on the report, Dr Andrew McCulloch of the UK's Mental Health Foundation said, 'The mental health of our young people is a critical issue: cases of anxiety and depression have risen by 70% over the past twenty-five years, and up to 60% of adolescents with a mental health problem will carry that through into adulthood.'[8]

As I suggested earlier, these issues cut right across family, class and ethnic backgrounds. They can't be explained by families in poverty; nor by the rise in divorce and single-parenthood; nor by a small number of teenagers whose problem behaviour is getting worse; nor by an increase in the rate of reporting such problems. The Deputy Director of the Nuffield Foundation, who funded the 2004 research on adolescents' mental health, said: 'It's not a small tail pulling down the average, but a more widespread malaise.'[9]

The Nuffield study focused on the general experience of adolescents, and did not look specifically at more extreme concerns such as the incidence of self-harm and suicide. But these dramatic symptoms of teenage insecurity are also on the rise. A 2006 report by the Mental Health Foundation called *Truth Hurts* finds that self-harm 'is a hidden epidemic of horrific proportions, and we know virtually nothing about why it happens or how to stop it'.[10] The young people interviewed for the report describe a range of factors that trigger their behaviour: being bullied, not getting on with parents, academic pressure and general stress. 'Adolescents who self-harmed were rare thirty years ago. Today, self-harming is a dramatic, addictive behaviour, a maladaptive way for growing numbers of youngsters to relieve their psychological distress,' says adolescent psychiatrist Dr Dylan Griffiths. Of the 160,000 people treated for self-inflicted injuries in hospital emergency departments in England in 2005–6, 24,000 – 15% – were aged between fifteen and nineteen. South Staffordshire NHS Trust has run a pilot scheme that allows self-harmers to cut themselves under the supervision of nurses.

That our children are behaving in such self-destructive ways calls out for explanation. Experts suggest that self-inflicting pain is a short-term, desperate way of over-riding other feelings that seem confused and irresolvable. For some people sharp pain can drag them into the present, and force all other nagging anxieties out of the loop of consciousness – for a while. One teenage boy described his self-harming like this:

> It was a way to get rid of the hurt and anger. But the rush it gave, the sense of feeling better, was so short-lived that I had to do it many times . . . I don't know how to release my feelings in any other way.

A teenage girl said:

> I was twelve years old when I began, and pretty depressed, angry and isolated. One day I accidentally hit my hand really hard against my bed, and experienced this sudden feeling of relief. Then I decided to cut myself, to see if I could make the good feelings last longer. I began cutting myself once a week on average . . . It became the only way I could keep going.[11]

The summer of 2007 saw an outbreak of 'tombstoning' across the UK. Tombstoning involves jumping off high rocks into the sea, or off bridges into rivers. It is most popular amongst teenage boys. It is very dangerous – that is the point – and several hundred have been injured and the first fatalities have already occurred. Why do they do it? sixteen-year-old Jez explained, 'You spend the whole day in school doing boring stuff and [wanting] to do something that will give you a rush. Jumping does that. Just for a second you forget all the boring bits of your day and feel free.' Eighteen-year-old Steve said, 'It's a way of getting out of your mind for a moment or two without taking drugs or drinking alcohol. When you're out there in midair you don't think of anything – your head goes clear. And then you hit the sea and you feel so alive.'[12] Having a bit of fun is one thing. Needing to risk your life in a desperate attempt to find a few seconds' peace of mind is quite another.

Another 2005 report, based both on interviews with 1,000 12–19-year-olds and an analysis of national statistics, claims that 900,000 adolescents have been so miserable they have contemplated suicide. Childline, the children's charity and helpline, report a 27% increase in calls from suicidal youngsters from 2005 to 2006.

What is making young people so insecure?

Family life for many young people, regardless of race or class, is often complex and unstable. Only the lucky ones now have a supportive extended family, and many have experienced family break-ups. Step-parents and half-siblings may have to be accommodated. Children of divorced parents shuttle between Mum and Dad, involving repeated adjustment to their different life-styles and values. Kids act up or may seem to take things in their stride; either way, it's hard work, requiring levels of sophisticated emotional intelligence that the bland work on self-esteem in their PSHE (personal, social and health education) lessons may not even begin to touch.

As a result, friendship groups have become more central to identity. Social life outside the home begins earlier, and access to drink, drugs and sex becomes correspondingly easier. These cross-currents create frequent opportunities for conflict, as neither parents, teachers nor the young people themselves quite know where the boundaries should be drawn. Ann Hagen, editor of the *Journal of Adolescence*, sums it up: 'At fifteen or sixteen there is a real struggle ahead [about] how you are going to succeed and get settled. We have high expectations of responsibility, independence and academic achievement of our teenagers without the other side of the equation: giving them the means to achieve that.'[13]

Young people live in a world of fierce yet fragile allegiances, in which consumer products are the ephemeral badges. In liking, choosing, buying, possessing and displaying, they fill in precious details of who they are, and where their allegiances lie. Which football club to support? Which band to listen to? What clothes to wear? Whether to have sex (or pretend to have done) and who with? All such choices can be a matter of social life and death. Many teenagers' days are filled with a series of choices and potential pitfalls in which their every utterance can be fraught with the possibility of Getting It Wrong.

Risk-taking is often one of the prices of admission to a social group. To be deemed daring, to damn the consequences, not to mind about possible hurt to yourself or others can lead to being in with the right group. Young people have always wanted to take risks: to defy the dull, sensible advice of their elders. In the good old days young men were sent off to war, to get it out of their system, or to die. Now we see the risk-taking every weekend on an epidemic scale: drink, drugs, unprotected sex, fighting, racing stolen cars. The idea that it's cool not to care, not to be touched or affected, can be tested and displayed through collective risk-taking, or even by your vicarious reactions to increasingly extreme horror movies or porn. The trick is to keep joking and laughing, whatever atrocity or obscenity is on the screen.

Best friends are absolutely vital, but the shadowy threat of falling out, or of a breach of trust, deliberate or inadvertent, can constantly hover in the background. And moving between different groups and contexts demands constant readjustments of personality, in order to fit in. Many young people even keep a stock of subtly different accents for different social contexts. And despite their best efforts there is a continual risk of a collision between the different compartments of their social worlds.[14]

A safer – but still exciting – kind of intimacy, and test-bed of identity experimentation, is instantly available online. Chat-rooms allow young people to experiment with their identity in ways that can become both thrilling and addictive. The chat-room vastly expands the opportunity to shed unwanted aspects of their real, burdensome bodies and personalities – the nose they don't like; the self-consciousness they hate

– and invent alternative identities that, so young people say, can feel very real.

To be a teenager today, is to be a shape-shifter and a quick-change artist, and there is pleasure and risk, but also stress, in that freedom. Behind all this sophisticated semi-conscious role-play, nags the question 'But who am I *really*?'

The culture of celebrity in which we are all immersed invites young people, as it does the rest of us, to gossip and judge, rather than think and learn. Teenagers are continually buttressing allegiances and identities by expressing choices, judgements and preferences about people in the news and on television. The fascination with celebrity invites naïve dreams of easy success, and facile judgement without consequence. Adolescents need (and want) people to admire, to look up to. They want people to be like. If they are lucky, they will find relatives, family friends or teachers who embody positive values well enough to inspire their respect. If not, and they turn to the media for their role models, they will see people winning money by chance or through the accumulation of trivial facts, foul-mouthed footballers and rock stars earning huge sums of money, Page Three girls notorious for their drug habits or plastic surgery featured in newspapers, models with eating disorders gracing the front of magazines, dishonest politicians lying to the people who elected them. What can we hope they will learn from the examples being elevated in the press and on television? While some of the activities of these celebrities may be condemned it certainly does not stop them being stars. Adrift in this moral maelstrom it is not surprising that young people seem to flip between apathy and passionate idealism.

Religion in all its forms responds to that idealism, and it may also offer an escape from the burden of being personally responsible for dealing with so much complexity. The flight into fundamentalism is a flight from complexity and responsibility – and a time-honoured and venerable one it is too. Teenagers' idealism, their quest for something that is of ultimate concern, is wonderful, but it also makes them vulnerable. Escape from responsibility and uncertainty is offered by a whole host of religious cults and spiritual clubs. But in the spiritual supermarket, there are good, bad and indifferent products, and for young people who are not encouraged to question and challenge it might not be easy to tell from the packaging which is which.

And to compound these worries is the truth that for many young people adolescence is lasting longer as financial worries are reinforced by the prospect and then the reality of debt. Funding university education and getting on the housing ladder are both daunting prospects. As a result, financial dependence on parents lasts longer – the average age of leaving home has risen to around twenty-four. What used to be the major life step or right of passage of 'leaving home' is increasingly reversible, as young adults come and go.

What do young people say about their world?

What do young people themselves say about their lives? How do they view the future? What do they expect of adulthood and the world of work? One major survey of 3,500 young people, aged between eleven and twenty-five, was carried out by the Industrial Society (as it then was, now the Work Foundation) in 1997. The report is more than ten years old, but I think we can safely expect the conclusions to be, if anything, even more valid now than they were then.

> Most [young people] fear that their world will generally become more challenging, and some have a bleak view of future opportunities and trends . . . Their lives are riddled with insecurity, and traditional aspirations seem inappropriate in the context of the world as young people experience it . . . At school, they are told that they need qualifications in order to get a good job . . . meanwhile, media reports and the experience of unemployed family and friends suggest that job security is an illusion . . . Many young people look to the market to seek forms of escape: acquiring clothes . . . and other 'badges of belonging' as well as using drugs. The youth drug-dance culture is largely young people's attempt to create an alternative world.

The theme of insecurity recurs time and again in the report. More than half (63%), felt that school did not prepare them for life in the real world. Three-quarters of all 11–25-year-olds, and 85% of all young women, were afraid of being physically attacked. Only one fifth of all young people said they felt part of their local community. More young people said they felt part of their friendship group than they did of their family. Less than half felt part of their school.

And the UK's young people are not alone in these feelings. A recent study of 650 Australian teenagers' views of the future concluded:

> Many of the young people in this study expressed a strong sense of negativity, helplessness, despondency and even anguish about the anticipated problems facing their society and the world at large. For a majority, [their perceptions] ranged from intensifying pressure and competition in schools . . . to worsening trends of physical violence and war, joblessness and poverty, destructive technology and environmental degradation.[15]

The words used by those young people to describe the future included *uncaring, violent, unfair, mechanised, unsustainable* and *corrupt*.

School is stressful

With all the uncertainties, responsibilities, complexities and choices of their out-of-school lives throbbing away in the background, academic pressure turns up time and again as one of the prime causes of young people's feelings of stress and apprehension. UK Government concerns with standards and accountability have led to teenagers being tested virtually to destruction. Young people are continually urged to study hard, and told how important their results will be.

Whatever it may say in the school prospectus, the message of the educational medium is clear: success means getting enough points at A-level to get onto the university course you want. By that yardstick, three out of every four young adults are going to fail. How they interpret and cope with that is going to be crucial. Their family and peer group, as well as the personal resources they have managed to develop, will count for a good deal. But, as Ann Hagen says, boosting their level of resilience is not something that many schools currently know much about. Students are rarely coached, effectively and systematically, in the habits and qualities of mind that will enable them to meet these demands with confidence. At best they are given revision guides and mock exams.

So even many of the 'good' schools are contributing to the demands and stresses placed on young people rather than to the development of their personal resources. Calls to Childline by young people struggling to cope with the pressure of exams have shot up in the last few years. Childline's Chief Executive, Carole Easton, says:

> Exam stress affects almost every child at some point in their education. Everyone who cares for and works with children needs to look out for warning signs that a child may be struggling to cope with exams . . . Some children who call Childline tell us that exams are the 'last straw' in their young lives.[16]

Even the head of the UK Qualifications and Curriculum Authority, Dr Ken Boston, says 'the assessment load is huge. It is far greater than in other countries, and is not necessary for the purpose'.[17]

This irony has not gone unnoticed. The Children's Commissioner for England, Sir Al Aynsley-Green, commenting in the wake of the Unicef report, attributed a good deal of young people's stress to the constant pressure of school tests, and the lack of a curriculum that addresses their concerns. 'Children feel under such pressure from endless testing, they do not feel they have the time to enjoy themselves,' he explained. 'What is the purpose of education? Is it for the attainment of government targets, or is it to provide children with the life skills to become confident adults?'[18]

Aside from exams, schools are stressful places for young people for a host of familiar reasons. They worry about not being liked, not fitting in, falling out with friends. They worry about not being able to cope with the weight of homework that they are expected to do. They worry about being picked on by teachers; about not knowing the answer to questions; about looking stupid; about being laughed at. They worry about being bullied – as they move up from primary to secondary school, the fear of being bullied is their number one anxiety. They feel vulnerable on the unsupervised journey between home and school.[19]

While young people are struggling to reconcile the twin pressures both to stand out and to fit in, school has traditionally ignored that struggle, and stood them in a long straight line labelled 'achievement' that graded them from the 'weakest' to the 'brightest', reducing their desire to be rich and variegated to a single dull dimension. Now, schools *say* they are interested in 'personalising' learning to suit individuals, but the message of the medium has not changed very much. At sixteen, young people will still be made to find their place in that line, which remains the essential benchmark of the school's success, as well as that of each individual. The only individuality that gets official recognition can be expressed in subject choices, and the school's university report.

The stress of school is compounded, for many youngsters, by their inability to see the point of it. The report from the Work Foundation cited earlier sums up children's feelings thus: 'Schools are seen by young people as failing to equip them with the ability to learn for life, rather than for exams.' A third of 11–16-year-olds interviewed were bored by school. Here are some typical quotations from the interviews.

> The things you learn in school . . . you're not really using them in actual real life . . . I think there's a gap. In school everything works like clockwork. You know, you go to your lessons, you do your work, you learn all your information and it sticks in your head, you do your exam and you get all the information you can possibly get. Real life is not like that. (eighteen-year-old man, Leicester)
>
> You learn to read and write in the Infants and Juniors – and then the rest of it, to be honest, most of it I can't even remember now. (twenty-two-year-old woman, London)
>
> While you're in school you're expanding your brain. Outside of school and in work you're learning about life. Simple as that. (twenty-three-year-old man, London)

Moving from the problem to the solution

Overall, it is an unusual teenager, these days, whose world is not full of demands, risks and opportunities, all of which are hard to assess. The mental and emotional demands of modern life are intense, and not surprisingly, young people (like their parents) often feel in over their heads.[20] What all this uncertainty and complexity amounts to is a huge learning demand on young people. They are faced with complicated, ambiguous predicaments on a daily basis. They are expected to make numerous choices and judgements, often on the basis of inadequate information. In every sphere, the social as much as the intellectual or practical, they have to weigh evidence, ask questions, discuss options, check the trustworthiness of different sources of information and advice, try things out, make mistakes and try again, imagine 'possible selves' they might become, take other people's views into account and sometimes stand their ground. Outside of school as well as within, their lives are roller-coasters of sophisticated learning. And as the traditional sources of guidance and authority are often weak and conflicting young people are left feeling individually responsible: as if, as one teenager said, 'I am continually having to make it up as I go along,' always in danger of screwing up and looking stupid.

In a nutshell, young people are stressed. Psychologists tell us that 'stress' is what happens when the demands made on you exceed the resources you have to meet them. A continuing imbalance between demands and resources leads to feelings of being inadequate, anxious and out of control. Under these circumstances, people feel obliged to try to manage their feelings rather than to focus on tackling the demands themselves. And this leads to denial, withdrawal, blaming, escapism and displacement activities. To put it simply, getting drunk, depressed or aggressive are increasingly desperate attempts to avoid the self-criticism that comes from not feeling up to dealing with life's problems.

What the review in this chapter shows is that the range and weight of the demands on young people are intense, and they have little scope for reducing them. They cannot change their family structure, they cannot change the nature of youth culture, they cannot turn off the clamour to spend and consume, they can't change educational legislation or remove GCSEs. So they are left with only two options: to work on developing their resources; or to engage in displacement activities – the self harming, the fantasies, the procrastination or the fundamentalism.

Some of the resources that can reduce young people's stress will be social and economic. Mentors can help, and so can better facilities. But at their heart the key resources are psychological: they are the abilities and traits which enable us to meet difficulty calmly and capably. The key resources, in other words, are those of the confident learner.

- If you are curious – if you are able to engage with new challenges and investigate them – you are more likely to expand your capacity to cope than if you are passive and apathetic.
- If you are resilient – if you can stick with difficult things and not give up at the first hurdle – you are more likely to find the solution.
- If you know how to balance your imagination and your logical mind, and to think things through with a mixture of creativity and clarity, you are more likely to come up with good ideas.
- If you can ask for help and receive feedback without getting upset, you will learn faster than if you are defensive or self-righteous.
- If you know how to take a step back, take a deep breath, and calmly think things though, you will solve problems more effectively than if you are impetuous.

All of this seems barely more than common sense. So why is no one in education talking about how these habits of mind can best be cultivated? Why is that vital third perspective – that of school as an apprenticeship in the craft of real-life learning – still continually eclipsed by sterile argument about content and qualifications?

Learning happiness

It is not just that learning power gives young people the tools to cope with uncertainty; learning is a deep and pleasurable urge in its own right. People seek out activities that will stretch and challenge them, be it the daily sudoku, a scuba dive, a holiday romance, a demanding book or a business deal. Young people are no different: they are inveterate and enthusiastic learners. They will work hard to pursue their projects and will spend hours practising their dance steps or their guitar chords, their joke-telling, their make-up or their computer gaming skills. They love the feeling of energy, absorption and satisfaction that such learning delivers (and many of them are acutely aware of the life-less quality of much of the learning they are required to do in school).

Surveys have found that 'happiness' is associated much more with the rewarding pursuit of non-trivial challenges than it is with having nothing to worry about.[21] Not having any challenge is an aversive state if prolonged, and people will go looking for trouble, or will make it if necessary, in order to create a challenge that they then have to rise to. Happiness is what parents say they want for their children. They want them to be safe, healthy and independent people who feel at home in the world; who can make and keep friends; who can face what life throws at them intelligently and cheerfully. Most parents are less worried about what form their children's lives take than about their mental and emotional well-being. They know that happiness has to do with purpose and passion rather than passivity; with the satisfaction of taking on real challenges and not running away from difficulty.

The solution to stress is clearly not Prozac or therapy. These responses may be short-term palliatives, but they do not tackle the root problem, which is the swamping of resources by demands. A British Medical Association spokesman has suggested that all adolescents be screened for psychiatric vulnerability. Lord Richard Layard of the London School of Economics has called for 10,000 more youth counsellors. Both of these are Band-Aid responses.[22] Some teachers wonder whether there is an alternative to this palliative approach, whether they could be doing more to narrow that yawning gap between what they know their students need, and what they are used to delivering. Could school really help young people develop the resources they will need, and so help them resist the superficial appeal of those stress responses? Is it possible to address such big themes practically and effectively, and not just get lost in a miasma of grandiose and woolly good intentions?

The fact that these are by no means new worries and ambitions, is demonstrated by this quotation dating from 1924:

> Greeting his pupils, the teacher asked:
> What would you learn of me?
> And the reply came:

How shall we care for our bodies?
How shall we rear our children?
How shall we live and work together?
How shall we play?
For what ends shall we live?
And the teacher pondered these words,
And sorrow was in his heart,
For his own learning touched not these things.[23]

Questions about the fundamental purposes of education have been around since schools began. If we are to make real progress in rediscovering the heart of education, it is to these fundamentals that we shall now have to turn.

2

What *is* the point of school?

School, I never truly got the knack of. I could never focus on things I didn't want to learn.

Leonardo di Caprio

School is under attack from all sides and for a range of reasons. Literacy rates, examination results and truancy are familiar pegs for discussions about the failings of schools, and are regularly revisited in the media. But other, deeper concerns are reflected in an increasing clamour of voices from across all ages and stations both within the education system and outside it. The professionals and students who spend their daily lives in schools are questioning the very basis of the system.

In this chapter we will first review the current success rate of schools using their own indicators, and then start to look below the conventional arguments and statistics to expose those deeper questions about its very purpose.

Literacy, exam results and truancy

Even on its own terms, education is hardly a success. Despite government claims, levels of literacy have not changed very much between the 1950s and 2007. An apparent improvement in performance over the first five years of the so-called 'literacy hour' turns out to be a reflection of teachers' success in preparing eleven-year-olds for national tests rather than a sign of a genuine increase in pupils' reading and writing ability. Estimates vary, but it seems that by the end of their compulsory eleven years in school, around 20% of young people still struggle with the basics of the three Rs. Almost 350,000 teenagers a year are failing to master the basics of English and maths. The 2006 review of basic skills in the UK headed by Lord Sandy Leitch found that one in six adults do not have the literacy expected of an eleven-year-old, and half do not have the equivalent level of numeracy.

Apart from literacy and numeracy scores at the end of primary school, the other major indicator of standards are the General Certificate of Secondary Education examinations, GCSEs. In 2007 just 44% of young people achieved what the government considers to be the baseline: five GCSE passes including English and maths. In other words, a majority of all students are leaving school without having achieved this most basic of benchmarks.

Intense pressure on schools by the government causes these statistics to go up (or sometimes down) by one or two percentage points a year. But this overall level of achievement is appalling, and these minor fluctuations are derisory. If we have not yet figured out how to educate young people in a way that enables the vast majority to feel they have gained something valuable, then that must indicate a basic fault in the system. School is dramatically failing, even at this most basic of tasks. Any manufacturer who consistently produced over 50% of rejects would not stay in business for long.[24]

Even many of those young people who have gained several good GCSEs and have gone on to A-levels and higher education, turn out to have very limited literacy and numeracy abilities. More than 50% of successful A-level candidates, and around 30% of those with a degree, only achieved a grade D-G in English at GCSE level (and such results count as a pass). The Confederation of British Industry has lost faith in GCSE exams because so many young people with GCSE passes are unable to function adequately in the workplace. The CBI's Director General Richard Lambert claims that one in three businesses are being forced to send staff (many of them graduates) for remedial lessons in basic literacy and numeracy.[25]

Another education 'vital sign' is the truancy rate. In 2005 a record number of students, 1.4 million, skipped school in England – despite the government's spending £885m over the previous seven years on a raft of measures to try to get the truancy rate down. That's 55,000 missing youngsters every day. Truanting jumped by 10% over the previous year. Almost a quarter of students in inner city schools were absent without apparent reason for up to a week each year. There were 215,000 'persistent absentees' – that is, those who were away for six weeks or more. The chair of the House of Commons public accounts committee, worried about the wasted millions, said: 'The DfES is losing ground in its battle against truancy.'[26]

There are obviously many reasons why youngsters play truant, but one, surely, is that they do not perceive the relevance and value to their own lives of what is being offered and are less willing than they would have been twenty or fifty years ago to meet this with docility and deference. Without a story that makes sense to them, today's young people are not going to buy in to what school offers, and they are more likely to disengage – some of them quietly, some disruptively.

Conversely, if they understood how attendance at school could cumulatively build their capacity to cope with life as they experience it, and as they accurately anticipate it will be, I believe the vast majority would turn up and do their best. Every teacher I know can tell stories about how sullen young people are magically transformed into intelligent and committed learners when something engages their interest and fires their passion. Confusing disengagement with lack of ability is one of the most dangerous mistakes a teacher or a school can make.

Deeper criticisms of schools

The experience of students

So the statistics tell us that failure is rampant, and half of all young people are failing at the qualifications game. It is neither productive nor accurate to shrug this off as their fault – to suggest that the problem is lack of motivation or ability on the part of the students. For at a deeper level school, as we shall see, is failing all students – the apparent successes as well as the more obvious failures.

Examination performance is not the only criterion against which to judge the success of schools. Exams only reveal what knowledge young people were able to display on a particular day, after plenty of revision. And they don't tell you about other, more abiding interests, understandings or capabilities that students may have developed. Yet, if education is a preparation for future life, the development of such inclinations and qualities is vitally important. Unfortunately, not much data is collected on this. But there are one or two studies that ring some very loud alarm bells.

The National Foundation for Educational Research has evaluated the effect on children's reading of ten years of the National Literacy Strategy. They have found that levels of reading *ability* have indeed risen over that period, as the government claim (though, as we've seen, a good deal of that seems to be down to 'teaching for the test'). But there is a cost. Levels of reading *enjoyment* have gone down – and this despite the Harry Potter phenomenon. Pleasure in reading fell most dramatically for eleven-year-old boys – from 70% who enjoyed reading stories in 1998 to 55% in 2003. Over this period girls' reading enjoyment held up better – but since 2003, their pleasure in reading stories has dropped to nearer the boys' level.[27] In the obsessive pursuit of 'standards', the pleasure of reading has been damaged, perhaps irreversibly.

Is this collateral damage to the pleasure of reading a cost that we can afford to bear? The Progress in International Reading Literacy Study, PIRLS, is a huge project monitoring the levels of literacy worldwide. The latest evidence from PIRLS, published in 2006, shows that 'reading for pleasure outweighed every social advantage, including parent's income, in the future success of the child'.[28] Children's success in life depends not on whether they *can* read, but on whether they *do* – and derive enjoyment from doing so. So it not just that damaging the disposition to read deprives young people of the pleasure of curling up with a good book; it shoots the fundamental purpose of education in the foot.

It is not just the disposition to read that seems to be undermined by current approaches to schooling. In studies at the University of Bristol, my colleagues Patricia Broadfoot, Ruth Deakin-Crick and I have found that students' perceptions of their own effectiveness and confidence as learners drops significantly from Key Stage 2 to Key Stage 3. Thirteen-year-olds see themselves as less resilient, less resourceful, less curious and less good at team-work than do nine-year-olds.[29]

Though we cannot be sure what the causal factors are, it is surely worrying that after a crucial four years of education, young people see themselves not as more capable and enthusiastic learners, but as less. It is possible that this slump happens quite quickly when young people enter secondary school. In a study of 1,000 young people in the city of Nottingham, the New Economics Foundation has found a dramatic drop in 'their ability to be curious and engage in challenging and absorbing activities' within a matter of weeks after entering secondary school.[30]

At a conference recently a headteacher approached me, keen to tell me a story. The previous evening she had been chatting to her daughter, a bright young woman doing some last minute revision for her A-levels. She asked her daughter what she thought she had really learned from her schooldays. The daughter thought for a bit and said: 'Be nice to the hard kids.' Her mother suggested that there must be more than that. The daughter thought some more and then said: 'Yes, I've learned I'm not very clever.' Telling me this story, the headteacher said: 'And I could have wept.' She thought it was a tragedy that this perfectly intelligent young woman should think that a sense of her own inadequacy was the second most important thing she would take away from her education.

Even successful students are failing to learn how to learn for themselves or to learn for pleasure. Worse, they may, like this young woman, pick up beliefs that sap their own confidence. There is abundant evidence that many successful students quickly become brittle and insecure when confronted with real problems they can't immediately solve. A classic study by Carol Dweck of Stanford University, for example, gave a mixed-ability class of students a maths test in the form of a booklet of problems. Some of the students were given a booklet that included, in the middle pages, a set of problems that were too hard for any of them to be able to do, even the high-fliers.

Dweck found that the students who had this experience of being stumped did worse on the do-able problems that came after than those who did not; and the group which was hit hardest were the normally high-achieving girls. Not being able to do something knocks their self-confidence so badly that they lose the ability to solve problems that would normally have given them no difficulty at all. Their achievement is high, but their resilience is fragile. When they don't know what to do, they go to pieces.[31]

As one bright fifteen-year-old girl, put it: 'I guess I could call myself smart. I mean, I can usually get good grades. Sometimes I worry though that I'm just a tape recorder repeating back what I've heard. I worry that once I am out of school, and people don't keep handing me information with questions, I'll be lost.'[32]

Some researchers are finding ways to help less articulate students show us how schools are failing them. Elizabeth Cooper works in a special school for children and young people with so-called 'moderate learning difficulties'. She is also studying for a masters in education at Bristol University, and for her research project she compared the way those young people went about learning, and the way they saw themselves as learners, in their normal school, with how they felt and behaved on a regular placement in a 'forest school', in the woods, where they worked together on practical projects. In the woods, they were different people. They were dramatically more confident, resourceful, collaborative, concentrated and thoughtful. And they saw themselves as such. Their apparent 'ability' – intellectually and verbally, as well as socially and practically – improved dramatically. They were interested, absorbed and relaxed, and so, cleverer. This research focused on the success of a possible alternative to school as we know it, but also succeeded in highlighting how mainstream school was failing these students.

There are thousands of bright, willing, successful people who do or did hate their schooldays. From Leonardo di Caprio's quotation at the beginning of this chapter to Winston Churchill's 'The only time my education was interrupted was while I was at school,' a quick Google search will bring up hundreds of expressions of disaffection or contempt for school. When I asked the fourteen-year-old son of a fellow professor at Bristol University to suggest a title for this book, he unhesitatingly offered *School Sucks*. This strong, well-documented chorus of disapproval cuts across history, race, gender and class. It cannot be written off as the losers' lament.

The findings of a MORI poll carried out for the Campaign for Learning in 2000, 2002 and 2004 could reveal part of the problem. The poll asked over two thousand 11–16 year olds to name the three most common activities in their classrooms. Number one across all three surveys was 'copying from a board or a book', selected by an average of 60% of the sample. It is worth noting that the situation is actually deteriorating as 'copying down' rose from 56% in 2000 to 61% in 2004. Two of the other most common activities were 'listen to the teacher talking for a long time', and 'take notes while my teacher talks'. The least likely thing to happen in a classroom according to the students surveyed was 'learn things that relate to the real world'.

The views of headteachers

In 2005, a hundred of the most successful headteachers in England were invited to attend a conference organised by the national Qualifications and Curriculum Authority, the QCA, with the aim of thinking about 'A Twenty-First Century Curriculum'. After agreeing that education is essentially a preparation for the future – the future of society, and the future of every young person – I asked them, in terms of this fundamental purpose, how they thought schools were doing. I gave them four options:

a We are achieving this aim already for the majority of youngsters.
b We would achieve it, if currently mooted reforms were success-fully implemented (and I allow them to choose their own favourite reforms to think about – foundation schools, synthetic phonics, fewer tests, whatever).
c We are a long way from achieving this goal – but at least you personally have a pretty clear idea what needs to happen.
d We have a long way to go, and you are not at all clear how we are going to do it.

There were no votes for A, none for B, about forty for C and about sixty for D. Not one of these thoughtful, successful headteachers, from all phases of the educational system, believed that the issues that are generating so much heat in the newspapers, and so much passion amongst politicians, went to the heart of the matter.

Over the last ten years or so, I have carried out this informal survey with over 8,000 people, all of them involved in some way with schools: student teachers, advanced skills teachers, advisers, inspectors, educational psychologists, governors and parents – as well as many more headteachers. Overall, I have got a few more votes for B, but only around 3%. The only time I got a radically different response was from the staff of a secondary school in the West Country, who told me later that they were reluctant to say what they really thought in front of their headteacher!

Everyone in education seems to know that the current reforms are not getting to the heart of the matter, yet publicly we carry on as if they mattered terribly. Or, to put it the other way round, it is as if we hold the basic institution of school in such reverence that we simply cannot conceive of ever doing more than tinkering with it. To think as deeply as we need to can feel almost like sacrilege. You can't help but be reminded of the old story of the man on his hands and knees underneath a street light. A helpful passer-by asks him what he is doing and he says he is looking for his car keys. 'Where did you lose them?' says the stranger. 'Down that alley-way over there,' says the man. 'But it is dark down there. This is where the light is.' We have to dare to go down the alley, if we are to find what education has lost.

Views from outside of schools

Some might find it unsurprising for students to be disaffected, and might even expect teachers and headteachers to be somewhat critical of their professional world. However, the malaise does not stop there. Senior figures from outside education share the same concerns.

Sir Christopher Ball became Director of Learning at the Royal Society of Arts and founder of the Talent Foundation after having served with the Parachute Regiment, lectured in mediaeval literature and been Warden of Keble College Oxford. With this wealth of professional and personal experience he had this to say in his Presidential Address to an Oxford conference on 'Globalisation and Learning':

> Our National Commission on Education [has] recently reported that after more than a century of compulsory education almost 15% of school-leavers and adults have limited literacy skills. An even larger proportion, 20%, of adults have limited numeracy skills . . . Faced with such challenges, old-fashioned 'national curricula' are not sustainable. They appear to be open to the remarkable charge of being both useless and ineffective.

In the course of his address, Sir Christopher quoted from the report of a recent conference organised by the prestigious Club of Rome:

> Our traditional and inherited systems of education and training have failed . . . A world containing almost 900 million adult illiterates is not the 'learning world' which is our vision. In the twenty-first century, those individuals who do not practise life-long learning will not find work; those organisations which do not become learning organisations will not survive; those schools, colleges and universities that do not put their students first will not recruit . . . What is required is not more of the same. If we are to reach the unreached and include the excluded, more must mean different.

Professor David Hargreaves, former head of the Inner London Education Authority, later Chief Executive of the UK Qualifications and Curriculum Authority, has similar concerns. In 2004 Hargreaves chaired a panel commissioned by the then Minister for School Standards, David Miliband, to advise on education. The panel concluded that schools should be focusing on 'enhancing students' capacities to learn and their motivation to learn' – and that this was not happening anything like broadly or effectively enough. When schools lose sight of this imperative, Hargreaves concluded, 'students pay a personal and social price for the resulting disadvantage'.[33]

Historical perspectives on schools

When you start to review the kinds of criticisms that are made of education, you quickly discover that there is very little that is new. The
concerns about levels of literacy, about the pressure of exams, about
teaching methods that dull the mind and spirit, the disconnection
from life, go back more than a hundred years. Quotations from the
Daily Mail and *Daily Mirror* of the mid 1970s have a remarkably familiar ring to them:

> The brutal truth is that standards have fallen.
> Individual acts of classroom violence that you read about –
> frequently you may think – do not, even so, represent the real
> scale of the problem.
> Most parents and many teachers believe that children are less lit-
> erate and numerate than they were twenty years ago.
> Literacy in Britain is marching backwards.
> General educational standards have slipped remarkably in the
> last decade or so.[34]

As long ago as 1856, educational reformer Joseph Payne was deploring
the habit of incessant testing – of, as he put it, 'continually pulling up
the plants to see the condition of the roots, the consequence of which
was that all good natural growth was stopped'. And, in contrast to the
regime of testing, and consequent teaching for the test, that was pre-
dominant, he proposed instead that education aim at:

> awakening the [child's] mind to the consciousness of its own
> power by bringing it into vital contact with facts of daily experi-
> ence, cultivating by suitable exercises its faculties of observa-
> tion, perception, reflection, judgment, and reasoning, aiding it
> to gain clear and accurate ideas of its own; training it, in short,
> to form habits of thinking.

Note, by the way, that Payne's image of education is very far from
the image of the child-centred romantic, encouraging each little
flower to bloom in its own way. He uses words like 'cultivate' and
'train', and has a clear idea of the 'habits of thinking' that are to be

cultivated. Yet that disciplined training of the mind is also totally different from the arcane busywork of a Mr Gradgrind. We might even say that Payne was sketching out the way of the epistemic apprenticeship.

Payne's condemnation of the educational reforms of 1862 captures exactly what contemporary critics of the National Curriculum of 2008 are saying:

> We need no hesitation in pronouncing it to be mechanical in conception, mechanical in means, mechanical in results . . . Just in proportion as you substitute mechanical routine, drill and cram, for intelligent and sympathetic development of the child's powers, you shall fail in the very object you are aiming at. Making quantity not quality the test of your results, you shall fail in securing either quantity or quality. The experiment which has now been tried for ten years in England ought henceforth to take a place in the annals of education as an example to deter . . . [It is] a system which assumes the name without possessing the spirit of true education.

A school inspector colleague of Payne's reported that, across all his educational experience, 'children were not taught how to overcome difficulties themselves, for example to decipher an unknown word, [but] to rely upon the teacher'. The failure to cultivate such a simple, useful mental ability is as shocking today as it was then.

Compare Payne's lament with this from contemporary Harvard educationist Ron Ritchhart:

> We've come to mistake curricula, textbooks, standards, objectives, and tests as ends in themselves, rather than as means to an end. Where are these standards and objectives taking us? What is the vision they are pointing toward? What purpose do they serve? What ideals guide us? . . . Without ideals, we have nothing to aim for. Unlike standards, ideals can't be tested. But they can do something that standards cannot: they can motivate, inspire and direct our work.[35]

What should schools be like?

The biggest worry about schools, captured by critics from Joseph Payne to David Hargreaves, is not that they are failing in their own terms; it is that their terms of reference are antiquated and constricted. The problem is not ineffective means, it is inadequate ends. To get to the root of the problem we have to go back to the fundamental purpose of education, and ask what schools are for.

Education is meant to supplement the upbringing provided by families and communities with a more systematic preparation for the future. That preparation involves cultivating the knowledge, skills, habits, attitudes, values and beliefs that we think young people are going to need if they are to thrive in the world that we foresee them living in.

Young people themselves have a good idea of what they want from schools. Here are samples of young people's thoughts about 'The school that I'd like'.

> The school I'd like would be one whose primary aim was to teach me how to live . . . Today, academic knowledge has become the sole interest of many schools, and few [teachers] are daring enough to abandon the exam rat-race for the job of creating thinking, adult individuals. (Christa, sixteen)

> In secondary education today the emphasis is on passing exams. Half-educated children emerge from school clutching their exam certificates, having been filled to capacity with information . . . They believe themselves to be 'educated'. To some extent they are, I suppose. But are they better equipped to understand and live with their fellow human beings? Has their education encouraged them to think creatively and originally? [No: but] isn't that what education should be about? (John, fifteen)

> Just as a subject has become absorbing and interesting it is locked away until the next lesson and the mind is switched to a new wavelength for the next subject. This continual interruption makes the work boring and the pupil loses interest. In tomorrow's school the work will be continued until it is finished. (Janet, sixteen)

The people who write textbooks do not make mistakes, and the best way to learn is by your own mistakes. (Jennifer, fifteen)

I hope that all the schools of tomorrow will have much more time to work individually on subjects the pupils find interesting, and more flexibility in the weekly programme of lessons. (Gillian, fourteen)

This is a school! A place where people together learn to live together and love one another, where people learn to reason, learn to understand and above all learn to think for themselves. School was not invented just for little people to become the same as big people, but for the pupils to learn how to live and let live. (Judith, thirteen)

I don't think I would get on very well in my ideal school because I am too used to being told what to do. (Frances, fifteen)

And finally here is Kirsty, aged seven, bursting with good ideas despite some bad spelling:

I wold like a school that some times let you writ out work for other children in other schools . . . i think as I am a child that I now how other children feel and so I can make it eseyer for them . . . I think it wold be nice if we cold sugest things for ourselvs to do . . . id like us to have more natur lessons out side and id prefer not to keep together as animals don't come out wen thers lots of peopel.

The voices of these young people are entirely contemporary – yet they are drawn from entries to a competition in the *Observer* newspaper in 1967.

Reviewing the entries, Edmund Blishen said they 'amounted to an enormous, remarkably good-humoured, earnest, frequently passionate and, at best, highly intelligent plea for a new order in our schools. No one who read through all these words could have believed for one moment that here were children seizing an opportunity to cock a snook at the status quo, for the sake of the snook.' A common plea resounded through all the entries, cutting across age, ethnicity and class.

First and foremost, these young people wanted to *learn*, not just to sit and be told. And they yearned to feel that the learning they were doing was preparing them for the rigours and challenges of life. Blishen says:

> From all quarters of the educational scene it comes, this expression of children's longing to take upon themselves some of the burden of deciding what should be learnt, how it should be learnt; this desire to get closer to the raw matter of learning, not to be presented with pre-digested knowledge by teachers or textbooks; above all . . . they want a form of learning for which the word, for so many of them, is 'research'; they want to discover how to be responsible for themselves and their own ideas . . . The children seem to sense what their elders are slow to sense, that you enter the [real] world ill-armed if all you have done is to submit, to some degree or other, to a pre-determined course of instruction from which, in its nature, most of the excitement and surprise of learning are excluded. They want to take risks, intellectually and emotionally. They want to break down the walls of the school, to admit the wider world.

And little has changed since 1967 to make 'The School That I'd Like' a reality. There are now some schools and classrooms that approximate more closely to what the children were asking for, and there may be a few more now than there were then but overall student's experience of school has not changed very much in the last forty years.

Preparing for what kind of world?

If it is obvious that we should be preparing young people for their future, we need to think about what that future might be like, yet when I ask teachers what kind of world they believe they are preparing their students for they admit that they are unsure. The global balance of political and economic power, developments in technology, global warming, terrorism and war, are individually larger issues than we can imagine outcomes for, and combining them means we really can't predict what the future holds for our children.

Education professionals do foresee a range of problems and societal changes that will contribute to the development of an unstable and disconcerting world:

- Social regulation and social anarchy, in the face of declining community cohesion, and the disappearance of shame as a social regulator (you can only feel shame with people who know you and whose opinion of you matters).
- The effects of increasing long-distance travel, and the 24/7 society, on people's mental and physical health. Are we already chronically sleep-deprived, and is it getting worse?
- The increasing North-South global divide, the state of Africa and the risk of rebellion by the 'dispossessed'.
- The effect of the rise of women on the place and identity of men.
- The effect of living in a complex miasma of chemicals that the human body does not recognise or know how to deal with.
- The development of nuclear technology in the Islamic world.
- How to care for the increasing elderly population.
- Increasing competition for scarce resources.
- The decline of some religions and the rise of fundamentalism and the proliferation of cults.[36]

And following that, here are some of the 'subjects' that teachers think could form the basis of a curriculum that would prepare young people to thrive in such a complicated and uncertain world:[37]

- Human rights
- Statistics and probability
- Empathy
- Managing risk
- Negotiation/mediation
- Ecology
- How to think
- Epistemology
- Collaboration
- Literacy
- Global awareness
- Imagination

- Ethics
- Healthy scepticism
- Body awareness
- Neuroscience
- Resilience
- Creativity
- Will-power
- Giving and taking feedback
- Relaxation

The most striking thing about this list is that many of the items are not 'subjects' at all as we currently recognise them, but qualities, traits, values and habits of mind. And there is nothing at all on the list that represents a body of knowledge that can simply be mastered. The point of learning statistics is not to pass an exam, but to enable the students to intelligently estimate risks and likelihoods in their own lives. Learning about ethics should lead to wiser decision making in morally complicated situations.

The teachers whose responses created the list have clearly concluded that 'facts' are not what our young people need. As American social commentator Eric Hoffer put it:

> In times of change learners inherit the earth; while the learned find themselves beautifully equipped to deal with a world that no longer exists.

'Why should I go to school?'

So it is not just that we need a clearer purpose for education and better ideas about how to translate this purpose into all the practical paraphernalia of schooling. We also need to convert this aim into a message about school that young people and their parents find accessible, credible and inspiring. At the moment, however, we still cling to a number of myths about the importance of education that are largely unconvincing.

The least inspiring myth of all is that young people must go to school because it is against the law not to. Going to school 'because you have to' isn't a very compelling reason. It invites you to be behind that desk 'in name only', and to create for yourself alternative activities and reasons for being there – like making and negotiating friendships. It offers no route-map, no clue about where you are supposed to be heading, no understanding of what is expected or required of you, no idea about what 'doing it well' would look like. And, incidentally, it's not true that the law compels young people to go to school. The law says that you have to be educated appropriately between the ages of five and sixteen 'through regular attendance at school *or otherwise*'. Today there are around 50,000 young people in the UK who are being educated 'otherwise'.[38]

Probably the most common reason young people are given for going to school is 'you need to study hard, pass exams, get the grades, go to college or university, get a good job, and, at the end of it all, you will be happy'. This obviously doesn't wash for the 55% or so of youngsters who are not going to make it through this obstacle course. Many of them know, almost from day one, that this rationale is not going to work for them. They know that, despite all the rhetoric to the contrary, they are still likely to end up serving burgers, cleaning offices, or answering queries from irritable strangers about train times or stolen credit cards.

Young people know the stories about the Finnish teenage millionaires who invented texting, and the internet geeks who dropped out of school to make their millions. They are well aware of the many celebrities who achieved a measure of fame and fortune despite their failure at school.

They may have heard of a recent survey showing that the rising cost of university education means that graduates have to work for twelve years after leaving college before they begin to overtake the earnings of their friends who went to work at eighteen. They may have heard the 2006 winner of the TV show *The Apprentice*, Michelle Dewberry, when she said: 'I hated school, and there was no way I was going to university. I wanted to earn money and I had my own house at twenty-one when my friends were just starting to work.'

And conversely, young people know about the hard-working, well-qualified people, perhaps some in their own families, who were made redundant in their forties and are now working on a supermarket check-out. They know about the graduates who couldn't get a job, and the teachers who have retrained as plumbers because the work is less stressful and better paid. It is hard for young people to maintain faith in the delayed-gratification, 'good job' scenario in the face of these daily counter-messages.

But even those who hope to succeed at the Qualifications Game can have a problem with this rationale, because it directs their interests and energies away from the learning itself and puts all their attention on the result. Getting 'two As and a B' becomes the goal, and learning is the chore that you have to do more or less efficiently to get you there. Many 'bright' students develop an instrumental attitude towards their education that leads them to sacrifice their natural curiosity in order to learn for the test.[39] They learn how much you can write in thirty minutes; what kinds of titbits of erudition are likely to impress the examiners; how to revise for the test in the most effective way. They know that such learning is of little value or interest in itself. Their knowledge is often skin-deep, and their learning habits and attitudes are tied directly to the very specialised job of passing exams.

Another reason given for attending school is that in these globally cut-throat economic times, the country needs them to be part of a 'world-class, highly-skilled, adaptable workforce'. While this might be a good reason as far as the government is concerned, 'contributing to the national economy' is not a very inspiring reason to get out of bed and pack your school-bag on a cold February morning. The idea that children go to school to be shaped into serviceable cogs in a giant economic machine really doesn't do it for young people – nor, it is to be hoped, for the majority of their parents and tutors.

In fact, there is a good deal of doubt about the relationship between education and national economic performance. Measures of national economic success go up and down, and so do countries' positions in educational league tables, but these movements are not strongly yoked together. Between 1970 and 1995, for example, school students in the European Union as a whole outperformed their counterparts in the USA on a variety of educational measures; yet in the same period, the EU created eight million new jobs to the USA's forty-one million.

Between 1970 and 1998, enrolment in Egypt's primary schools grew rapidly to more than 90% while secondary enrolment rose from 32% to 75%, and entry to university education doubled. Over the same period, Egypt rose from being the world's forty-seventh poorest country to being the forty-eighth . At the other end of the wealth scale, Switzerland, one of the richest of the OECD countries, has the OECD's lowest rate of university attendance and graduation.[40]

The most traditional answer to the question 'Why go to school?' is the claim that it is just self-evidently good for young people to be introduced to the treasures of their cultural heritage. No-one, it is argued, can consider themselves to be 'educated' if they are not acquainted with Shakespeare, Mozart and the periodic table. There have to be special places where this treasury is methodically laid out for young people and where, for their own good, they have to go.

Of course, the accumulated knowledge, wisdom and experience of the past provides a wealth of interesting and important things to be studied. In our multi-cultural society, that wealth is an ocean that has to be massively reduced to fit into the pint pot of the school years. Much has to be condensed, and much left out. Both condensing and selecting are fraught with difficulty. When intricate knowledge is condensed, it risks losing almost all that is of value, and ends up as a weak summary. You may remember Woody Allen enthusing about a speed reading course he had taken. 'The course was amazing. I read *War and Peace* in an hour. It's about Russia.' Instead of developing appreciation and curiosity, the demand for 'coverage' often results, in practice, in 'teaching by mentioning'.

What pupils instinctively know is that the content itself is less important than what you do with the content. You can make learning history or maths a dull, tedious slog; or you can make it a vehicle for stretching students' powers of analysis, empathy and collaboration. Being forced to copy down notes about metamorphic rocks or the symbolic purpose of Macbeth's witches does not make you a better person. It practices the skills of accurate transcription and retention – which are not worthless, but are probably not the most important life skills for the twenty-first century – and leaves other, perhaps more useful, mental habits unstretched. You cannot 'teach' any knowledge without strongly influencing the *way* in which young people engage with it: what mental muscles they are exercising through that engagement. And it is the development of those habits of mind that matters most. British scientist Richard Dawkins summed it up when he said:

> What matters is not the facts but how you discover and think about them: education in the true sense, is very different from today's assessment-mad exam culture.[41]

Dull teaching runs the real risk not just of cultivating relatively useless skills, but of creating a resistance to any future contact with those precious subjects. Sadly, even teachers who are passionate about their subject can fall into this trap, if they have lost the sense, beyond the cherished exam passes, of what they are teaching these things *for*. They may not even understand that the question of deeper purpose is legitimate and vital for the many well-disposed young people whose interests and passions are very different from their own. They may have no concept of how difficult or plain dull other intelligent, good-natured people may find the very same things that they find fascinating. And they may therefore be unable to provide any further justification, when a student, perfectly legitimately, asks why they should bother. They may be genuinely bemused by such questions. The things they teach are, to them, self-evidently timeless treasures. It is precisely that assumption of 'self-evident' value that needs calling into question.

Counter-criticisms

In my work at conferences and in schools I have received three common reactions to my criticisms of current schooling, and the kinds of innovations which I am advocating.

The first is, 'We're doing all this already. It is just "good teaching".' That is partly true: some of these criticisms and ideas, as I have shown, are not new or even particularly complex. But much of what has passed for 'good teaching', though it may get the results, does so by creating young people who are docile, uncritical, unimaginative and dependent. Good teaching for the learning age is very different from 'effective spoon-feeding', and we need to be very clear about how they differ.

Second, people say 'It's impossible. Some kids are just not very bright, or they are just unmotivated and no amount of fancy ideas like yours will engage them.' I hope to convince you in chapters 5 and 6 that this concern, while understandable, is also unfounded. Words like 'low-ability' and 'lazy' are actually sloppy and unhelpful. They do not describe the problem; they are part of the problem. The fatalistic idea that education is a game at which a large proportion of young people are bound to fail is antiquated, untrue and unacceptable. Certainly, there are some young people who are suited by their background and their interests to take more naturally and successfully to the kinds of learning that school requires. But, as we have seen, that particular kind of learning is not the most powerful apprenticeship for learning in real life; and being an all-round powerful learner is not the same thing as being a good student. Not all are cut out for academic success, but all can get better at learning.

And third, people sometimes say, 'Well, it sounds interesting, but it's new and untried, and I don't want my child to be used as a guinea-pig in some professor's experiment.' However, we have to remember that conventional education is an experiment too – one which we have had good reason, for several decades, to question deeply. The *status quo* is not safe, and inaction is not a neutral option.

We have to conclude from this summary of current criticisms of education, that it is failing in terms of both its means and – much more importantly – its ends. The problems are real and deep. Too many young people fail to learn to read, write and count well enough. Too many leave school with a poor clutch of exam-passes and a sense of failure. Too many vote every day with their feet. But the solution is not to herd the truants back into school, and try to lever a few more across some statistically important threshold. The issues are more systemic: the traditional model of education is not fit for purpose – the purpose of sending young people off on their lives feeling confident that they can deal with the difficult things that life might throw at them. There is a lot of rhetoric about schools preparing children for

first response is to pile more pressure on schools to raise their exam results. New targets are set for schools, performance is checked, and failure to meet those targets brings a variety of punitive consequences. League tables of schools are published and parents are encouraged to believe that they can choose to send their children to a school with better results. In reality parental school choice is a bit of a myth, but the league tables do help to create 'desirable' and over-subscribed schools, and of course, 'failing' undersubscribed schools. As school budgets depend on the number of children 'on roll', market forces are used to hit schools that don't get good results in the pocket.

These crude reforms have a number of predictable results. Instead of being galvanised into action, staff morale is as likely to plummet in a school which has falling rolls, or has been identified by Ofsted, the school's inspectorate, as having 'serious weaknesses', or even needing 'special measures'. Additionally, with all the pressure to boost exam results, it is no surprise that creative headteachers find ways to improve their school's *apparent* levels of performance. The more important you make the achievement of measurable targets, the more people will find ways of massaging the figures. If young people are encouraged into easier subjects – by letting them drop say, physics or French – results can be made to look better. Weaker students can be entered for a General National Vocational Qualification, (GNVQ), which can count as the equivalent of four GCSEs, and the results will show another encouraging rise. Nine of the ten most improved secondary schools in 2005 achieved their success by entering greatly increased numbers of students for GNVQs, prompting the government to revise its 'key indicator' to require GCSEs in English and maths to be included in the statistics.

There is clear evidence from the Cambridge Review of Primary Education that this pressure has led to the curriculum being narrowed – subjects that are not subject to high-stakes assessment (like the arts and PE), and activities such as clubs and games, get squeezed out, and many schools and teachers find it impossible to resist 'teaching for the test'. In year six in primary schools, pupils say the fun goes out of learning and the anxiety levels of all concerned go up.[43]

Anxious parents boost the quality and sophistication of their children's homework and project work. While teachers, under pressure to improve results, are bending over backwards to nudge children over those statistically important thresholds. There are frequent claims that students are being coached as to what they need to do, and allowed multiple attempts at improving their coursework. One head of a school faculty, writing anonymously in the *Times Educational Supplement* has claimed that such leniency is now commonplace. It is a grey area, and many teachers are unsure just how much help they are 'allowed' to give.

Students themselves may find it hard to resist the temptation to do a little (or a lot) of downloading of prefabricated material from the internet. A *Times Higher Education Supplement* report recently showed that by the time students get to university, plagiarism is rampant. One in six undergraduates admit submitting work that is not their own. University of Kent sociologist Frank Furedi has claimed that university staff may even collude or turn a blind eye. Plagiarism can be hard to prove, generate a good deal of aggravation, and anyway, lecturers want their own results to look good. 'Cheating is now so rife on campuses that it is covertly accepted as part of the daily routine of British university life,' Furedi claims.[44] Even in school exams, blatant cheating is on the rise, up 27% from 2004 to 2005. Over 1,000 candidates were caught trying to smuggle their mobile phones into the examination room: 'phone a friend' has apparently gravitated from a game show strategy to an increasingly common exam ruse.

In the USA, an official report has documented the way in which the testing industry has responded to the pressure to assess by replacing essay-type questions with 'formulaic, machine-readable multiple-choice exams that are cheaper to produce and easier to mark'. These tests in turn encourage teachers to drill students in the low-level skills and bite-size facts that are all that is needed to do well on the tests, at the expense of more thoughtful learning and deeper understanding. Professor Dylan Wiliam, while head of research at the Educational Testing Service in Princeton said: 'Sanctions attached to failure are now so great that many teachers feel drilling multiple-choice questions is what they have to do.'[45]

The desire to have clear indicators of how well schools are doing, and to hold them accountable, is entirely sensible. What the British government seems to lack, however, is any understanding of human nature, and of how people's mindsets and motivations are shifted when they are forced to 'achieve targets' and publish 'key performance indicators'. Headteachers and GCSE students are not so dissimilar in the ways they react to 'high-stakes testing'.

Re-inventing school

In the drive for reform, the UK government has introduced a number of new kinds of school – particularly secondary schools – that are mostly old kinds of schools with new buildings, new cash or 'under new management'. City Academies, for example, invite private capital to sponsor new schools to replace struggling schools in inner-city areas. However, with a start-up cost of £30m or so per school, Academies are not (yet) looking like good value for money. Under the stricter criteria that include what are now called 'level 2' passes in English and maths, the performance of sixteen-year-olds at such schools looks less than impressive. Only 16% of Academy students managed 'five good passes' in 2005. Overall, they improved by 1.3% on the previous year, compared with a national average improvement of 1.7%. Two out of the three longest-running Academies actually did worse, on this yardstick, than the old schools they replaced. Seven Academies are in the bottom 200 state schools in the country.[46]

How schools appear to be doing can be dramatically different depending on which indicators are used to measure their progress. Under the laxer criteria where English and maths were not required, and GNVQs could be counted, Walsall Academy looked to be doing quite well, with 67% of students achieving the equivalent of five good passes in 2005. But under the more stringent criteria their 'performance' apparently plummeted, with just 7% achieving those five A-C grades at GCSE. One Academy was reported in its local paper as being so desperate for success that it has been offering GCSE students a cash handout of £150 if they get the magic five C-grades or better.[47]

Another new category, Specialist Schools, get more money if they can develop special expertise in one area of the curriculum such as sports, art or engineering. A typical school in the programme can receive around £600,000 on top of their normal funding over a four year period, so they ought to be delivering the goods. The statistics show they are indeed getting better GCSE and A-level results than the non-specialist schools. However the reasons for this are far from obvious, as a report by the Research and Information on State Education Trust (RISE) makes clear. A school can only gain specialist status if its exam results are already good. And the way they select their intake may have a huge part to play. There are strong suggestions that they are draining talented students away from other neighbourhood schools, to the increasing detriment of the latter (just like the old grammar schools). The RISE report concludes: 'Whether [their success] is due to their selection practices (overt and covert) or to their being already highly effective in order to gain specialist status is not clear. There is no proven causal link between the improved performance of these schools and their specialist status.'[48]

'Excellence in Cities', another costly scheme for improving education in the inner cities, launched in 1999, has, for its £386m, achieved no improvement in test results at ages fourteen and sixteen. An evaluation in 2003 by the National Foundation for Educational Research found no overall effect on GCSEs. Desperate for some crumbs of optimism, the DfES, who commissioned the research, pointed out that, in the most difficult schools of all, the maths results for fourteen-year-olds had gone up. The proportion of pupils reaching the required level rose from 1.1% to 1.9%: something to crow about, indeed!

Overall, these kinds of large-scale structural reforms turn out to be very poor value for money. But governments keep introducing them, because that is what governments do. Changes to the curriculum, the examination system, the methods of management and financing, the school-leaving age are the kinds of things that are amenable to central control. And announcing grand-sounding 'new initiatives' is what politicians like to do. The trouble is, such reforms leave the fundamental purposes and assumptions of education quietly in place. As long as we continue to measure 'success' predominantly in terms of examination performance, and to design curricula around pre-specified bodies of knowledge that have to be mastered, triumphant announcement followed by expensive disappointment will continue to be routine.

Occasionally someone does seem to spot that this approach is not working. Sir Michael Bichard was Permanent Secretary in the DfES (DfEE as it was then, DCSF as it is now) from 1995 to 2001. In the City of York Education lecture on 3 March 2006, he reminded the audience that David Blunkett had agreed in 1997 that school improvement should be about more than tinkering with the structures. 'Less than a decade later,' Bichard said, 'we are once again mired in a debate . . . which is essentially about structure. [And] as with any structural change, it consumes energy, causes uncertainty and can distract from the substance, while giving the impression, at least, that much is changing.' Indeed.

A brief history of educational 'reform'

There is no question that some changes to schools, over the years, have been for the better. Many school buildings are pleasanter, better equipped places than they used to be, corporal punishment has gone, and many more young people go on to university. Time and again, however, despite hard work and good intentions, these structural reforms do not quite get to the core of the problem they are designed to address. An incessant mass of legislation and a welter of theory and research has failed, so far, to produce a system that is fit for purpose. We should have learned the lesson of history by now – but hope continues to triumph over experience, and the tinkering goes on.

In the twentieth century we had, to name but a few, Board Schools, Elementary Schools, Grammar Schools, Secondary Modern Schools, Middle Schools, Technical Schools, Comprehensive Schools, Sixth Form Colleges, Special Schools and City Technology Colleges, and now we have, as well as many of these, Specialist Schools, City Academies and Trust Schools. Each restructuring is heralded as a great step forward, and each proves disappointing, and is superseded in its turn. Comprehensives, for example, were supposed to be great social levellers but the research soon showed that the rather romantic ideal of the rich social mix was undermined by the students' natural inclination to congregate into self-selected groups, thus, in many schools, reconstituting grammar and secondary modern 'tribes' under one roof. There are some parts of the UK where successive layers of restructuring co-exist, leaving local administrators with ten different kinds of school to manage, and an administrative nightmare. How can a comprehensive school be 'comprehensive' when it is competing with a traditional selective grammar school down the road?

The examination system also gets periodic makeovers that do little good. Written exams were going strong in 1900, and Examination Boards, smaller than, though very similar to, the ones we have today, have been in existence for a hundred years. The Dyke Ackland Report into examinations in 1911 expressed concerns very similar to those that still worry today's Qualifications and Curriculum Authority.[49] Between the World Wars, Matriculation metamorphosed into the School Certificate, which, in turn, evolved in the late 1940s into the General Certificate of Education at 'ordinary' and 'advanced' levels. 'O' levels were found to be too hard for less academic pupils, so in 1962 an easier version, the Certificate of Secondary Education, was instituted. But that came to be thought of as invidious, so in 1986 'O' levels and CSEs were amalgamated into GCSEs – with the predictable concerns about the 'brightest' not being stretched and the 'weaker' becoming demoralised. National Vocational Qualifications and General NVQs were introduced, designed to be 'different' from GCSEs, and then subjected to intricate arguments about how parity was to be established. 'A' levels were split into A2s and ASs, and the forms of the exams endlessly modified – but now 20% of entrants are getting A marks at A-level, though university tutors complain that these grades no longer identify the brightest and the best, so they have to set their own exams.

Even as I write, more demanding alternatives at the top end of GCSE (rather like 'O' level papers, perhaps?), and easier tests of 'functional English and maths' for the 'less able' are being reintroduced. There are suggestions – easy targets for the traditionalists to ridicule – that 'failure' is so demoralising for youngsters that their poor performance has to be rebranded as 'deferred success', or 'nearly'. Only around 2% of GCSE candidates actually fail, these days. But grades D and below are widely seen as not worth much, and below grade G is now called an 'entry level' qualification – not a fail – though nobody is fooled, especially not the students. An official enquiry has revealed that employers now find the intermediate GCSE grades B and C virtually worthless as a guide to a young person's mathematical abilities.[50]

Assessment by coursework has swung in and out of favour, depending on which of its pros and cons are most visible at the time. Compared with the intense pressure of written exams, which disadvantage the most stress-prone students, coursework offers a more leisurely and potentially creative way to show what you have learned. On the other hand, it is much harder to be sure that the finished product is all the student's own work. Back in the 1970s, before GCEs were phased out, there was briefly an option, called 'Mode 3', for schools to devise and assess their own courses of study, but that was seen as allowing far too much scope for 'subjectivity' (or cheating) and was soon dropped.

Two recurrent issues that are always hotly debated are class size and 'mixed ability vs setting'. We now know that neither of these is a magic bullet for raising standards. Class size only begins to make a significant difference when you get down to around fifteen per class, which is impossibly expensive for all but the best-endowed independent schools.[51] And the arguments about setting, banding and streaming, as opposed to mixed-ability teaching, should have been put to bed long ago, when it was discovered that the variable that made the most difference was not what method of grouping you chose, but whether the teachers who had to implement the system believed in it or not. Streaming gets the best results with teachers who believe in streaming; and mixed-ability likewise.[52] This unsurprising result does not seem to have brought the skirmishing to an end, even now. In their 1997 election manifesto, and again in 2005, the Labour government committed themselves to increasing setting, but have failed to deliver. Since 1997, the percentage of lessons taught in ability groups has actually fallen. A Conservative education minister was, predictably, 'shocked'.[53]

What of the actual content of the school curriculum? How has that fared? Astonishingly, it seems to have survived wave after wave of educational reform virtually unscathed. The 1904 Secondary School

Regulations required schools to teach English, mathematics, science, history, geography, a foreign language, drawing, physical exercise and manual work/housewifery. The list of subjects in the 1988 National Curriculum was identical, except that the last category was replaced with 'technology', drawing was changed to 'art', and music was added. The UK's foremost historian of education is Professor Richard Aldrich, and a more sober commentator on educational reform (or the lack of it) you could not hope to find. His comment on this lack of change? 'It is a shame upon us all that, at the end of the twentieth century, children in schools in England are following much the same curriculum as at the end of the nineteenth . . . The current list of subjects is no starting point for the creation of a national curriculum for the twenty-first century.' [54]

Aldrich points out the curious disconnection between the incessant rhetoric of educational reform and the monolithic inertia of the curriculum. Nowhere, ever, has the UK government taken the time to spell out the rationale that links, for example, the intention to 'prepare pupils for the opportunities, responsibilities and experiences of adult life', and the ten or so bodies of knowledge they are required to study. It is just presumed to be self-evident – which, of course, it is not at all. Politicians have behaved, says Aldrich, rather like a man who needs to get a train from London to Manchester, but ends up travelling to Leeds – because that is where his season ticket goes to.

Having centralised, dictated and examined the curriculum to an unprecedented extent, the UK government has now instituted some reforms that encourage schools to loosen the tight belt of the National Curriculum and create a distinctive identity, built around local conditions, interests and existing forms of experience and expertise. Current Secretaries of State for Education must have been reading old copies of the Tawney Report of 1931, which argued strongly that schools should evolve out of local initiative and experiment. 'There is no probability,' the report declared, 'that what suits Lancashire or the West Riding will appeal equally to London or Gloucestershire or Cornwall, and if education is to be an inspiration, not a machine, it must reflect the varying social conditions, and moral atmosphere, and economic conditions, or different localities.' Whether the current initiatives will have any more success at opening up the curriculum than did those of the 1930s remains to be seen.

When you look at this history, the overwhelming impression is of a system going round in circles, like a dog on a chain, endlessly trying to reach a bone that is out of its reach. Nowhere has Santayana's dictum that 'those who cannot remember the past are condemned to repeat it' been more amply demonstrated. The links of the 'chain' that stops deeper reforms are the assumptions that politicians cannot bring themselves to examine. We shall take a look at those links in the next two chapters. Meanwhile, we must conclude that a century of structural see-sawing has not produced the requisite improvement in the level of young people's engagement or achievement; and it has certainly not tackled the root problem of how to make them more confident real-world explorers.

Fool's gold: the false promise of 'brain friendly learning'

Tired of being restructured, pressured and told what to do by government committees, many teachers – perfectly aware of the need for reform – have taken matters into their own hands. What has excited the interest of many have been approaches that offer straightforward, practical things that busy teachers can do in their lessons to help young people learn more effectively. They include tools for organising and retrieving knowledge, such as 'mind mapping'; advice about how to help children get in the right state to learn, for example by sipping water; and ways of engaging different kinds of 'learning styles' or 'multiple intelligence' profiles.[55]

Often these hints and tips come with impressive-sounding justifications in terms of 'brain-friendly learning'. Organising what you know about the animal kingdom into a spidery diagram of connections (rather than into a dull list) is supposed to capitalise more effectively on the way the brain itself stores information. The encouragement to keep sipping water is based on the idea that a dehydrated brain learns less effectively. Dividing young people into different types of learners – for example, 'visual', 'auditory' and 'kinaesthetic' learning styles – is supposed to reflect differences in the ways their brains are wired. And providing a richer mix of visual aids, verbal explanations and practical activities is then supposed to allow each kind of learner to 'hook onto learning' in their own preferred way.

These techniques have appealed to many teachers, as they provide them with practical ways in which they can enliven the classroom, provide some welcome diversity, and they go down well with pupils. However, I have a number of concerns about these innovations.

First, the apparent science behind them has often turned out to be flawed. Many of the so-called 'learning styles' are far less permanent, pervasive or clear-cut than they have been claimed to be. Unsurprisingly, people change the way they approach things depending on what it is they are learning. I am a much more 'visual' learner when I am watching TV, more 'auditory' when listening to a teacher, and more 'kinaesthetic' when I am playing football – aren't you? Also, learning styles turn out to change and develop considerably over time. They are better thought of as temporary snap-shots of evolving habits and preferences than as life sentences.

It is also not true that the brain is a flexible 'plum' that is at constant risk of shrivelling up into a non-learning 'prune' if it is not kept moist by continual sipping. In fact, some research by Psychology Professor Peter Rogers, a colleague of mine at Bristol University, has recently shown that drinking water when you are not thirsty actually impairs learning.

Of course, being thirsty is a distraction; most children like being allowed their water bottle; and water is preferable to fizzy drinks.[56] I am not against the sipping of water in class but I am opposed to the needless misrepresentation of science, especially by people who want to sell something. Professional development for teachers is big business, and consultants and trainers are continually on the look-out for impressive, pseudo-scientific soundbites with which to wow their audiences. Teachers, keen to learn more about learning in order to teach their pupils better, are eager for such information. But they have neither the time nor the training to submit the claims of a confident-sounding presenter to the critical scrutiny they deserve. A recent study from Yale University shows that non-specialists are more likely to believe a bad explanation for something if it contains references to neuroscience.[57] Additionally, neuroscience is in its infancy. As American neuroscientist David Fitzpatrick said recently, 'Anything that people would say [about the brain] right now has a good chance of not being true two years from now, because the understanding is so rudimentary, and people are looking at things at such a simplistic level.'[58]

The second good reason to be a little sceptical is that, while much of this 'brain-friendly learning' is well-received, it doesn't actually make any difference to the results. I know of no good evidence that using mind maps or believing yourself to be an 'auditory learner' improves students' measured performance on anything. A major review of learning styles, for example, by a team at the University of Newcastle recently concluded that: 'Some of the best known and commercially most successful [learning styles tests] have such low reliability, poor validity, and negligible impact on pedagogy, that we recommend that their use in practice should be discontinued.'[59] Despite these misgivings, however, a DfES booklet recommending the Visual-Auditory-Kinaesthetic typology remains in circulation, and the Qualifications and Curriculum Authority continues to endorse the approach.

Another way of differentiating students that has proved very popular with schools uses the theory of 'multiple intelligences' proposed by Harvard University's Professor Howard Gardner. Instead of having just one pot of general-purpose 'intelligence', Gardner suggests that we all have eight different pots, one that is verbal, one mathematical, one spatial, one musical, one bodily, one interpersonal, one to do with self-awareness and one for dealing with nature. People are assumed to differ in their portfolios or profiles of intelligences, rather than just along a single dimension.

Yet Howard Gardner himself is very uneasy about some of the ways his work has been used in schools. On one visit to Australia he found a state-wide programme that claimed to be partly based on his theory. However, as he describes it, what he saw was 'a mishmash of practices – left brain and right brain contrasts, sensory learning styles, "neurolinguistic programming", and multiple intelligences approaches, all mixed up with dazzling promiscuity'.[60] And indeed the theory itself is not universally accepted. It has recently been criticised by Professor John White of the London University Institute of Education, who points out that Gardner's different pots of 'intelligence' map suspiciously neatly onto the classical school subject disciplines – which perhaps explains why teachers took to them so readily – rather than, as Gardner claims, onto different areas of the brain.[61]

The third reason for my scepticism of brain-based hints and tips is that many of them are too insignificant to provide the foundation for a renewed purpose for education as a whole. Knowing how to draw a mind map of your knowledge of football teams might make a tiny contribution to your real-world functioning – but mind mapping is surely not a powerful enough tool to help with the deep insecurities that we reviewed in chapter 1. It is not enough to have filled in a little questionnaire that convinces you that you are a 'kinaesthetic learner'. What is needed is a much more sustained attempt to grow those qualities of curiosity, resilience, imagination and reflection that are collectively going to give you the deep-down confidence you need.

Unconscious images that block reform

There is no shortage of people thinking about educational reform, yet the discussion remains at a superficial level. What is stopping it from going deeper? I think the problem is a couple of what linguists call 'dead metaphors', powerful images that drive, often unconsciously, our sense of what school is, and what it ought to be. [62]

Around 4,000 years ago, in both China and the Middle East, a model of education for children began to develop that was based on the kind of training provided for the priesthood. The priests were the intermediaries between the gods and the people, and in their training they learned God's Truth, and they also learned how to convey it to the populace with a certainty that brooked no dissent. This model of teaching and learning, based on the unquestionable authority of a few, high-status initiates, has echoed down through the ages. The tutors and professors of the mediaeval university, for example, adopted an only slightly secularised version of the monk's gowns and hoods, the same hierarchy of status, and also the same air of complete authority.

Knowledge was seen as eternal Truth, teaching its clear transmission, and learning its accurate memorisation. Knowledge in the classroom and the university, as in the seminary, was divided into separate disciplines – geometry, arithmetic, grammar and so on – and properly accredited teachers presided over this knowledge, dispensed it, examined it, and arbitrated over what was to 'count' as knowledge. The mediaeval grammar schools, and the great public schools of the eighteenth and nineteenth centuries, were built on this model. They were mini-universities for the sons of the gentry and the clergy. And they retained many of the trappings and assumptions of their monastic origins. The image of *school as monastery* persists up to the present, and the classrooms of Mesopotamia, 2500 BC, would be instantly recognisable to the students of today. Today's comprehensive schools have dropped the gowns and hoods, and somewhat broadened the curriculum, but this ghostly historical image still walks their corridors.

Even more evident in today's educational system in the image of *school as factory*. With the Industrial Revolution, education in the nineteenth century expanded from being an induction into power for the sons of the elite to an entitlement for the masses. And the root metaphor that drove that expansion was the production line. The resemblance between the organisation of school and the design of a factory is no coincidence. Even the architecture is similar. Mass production of literate, honest, punctual and dutiful workers was conceived of in exactly the same way as mass production of anything else.[63]

Within this imagined framework, education can be 'done' in the same way that a radio can be assembled. Production is concentrated in a special place and processes are standardised and replicated. Students are sent down the production line in batches, and a variety of 'technicians', each with an area of expertise – their 'subject' – adds one particular knowledge-component (of an 'educated mind') as they go. Batches can be arranged by age, and all students of a similar age are assumed to have roughly the same potential and to learn in the same way. Knowledge can be standardised, installed in manuals called 'textbooks', and chopped up into different sized bits – syllabuses, topics, schemes of work, and eventually the content of individual lessons – that can be bolted on, as it were, to students' minds bit by bit. Harder or more advanced components could only be fixed on successfully if the easier or earlier ones were securely attached already. Teachers might have a sense of the Big Picture, but students have no more need of the blueprint than does a radio. As in an efficient old-fashioned factory, everything can be specified, standardised and cut and dried. School years, terms, timetables, uses of space: all have to be predetermined and managed.

As on the production line, quality control is essential, so the 'products' are regularly tested and graded to make sure that the operations have been successful. If they are found to be faulty, it is usually because they are intrinsically so – 'low ability' or 'lazy' – or, more rarely, because the assembly-line worker, the teacher, is found not to be performing their operation properly. Occasionally revised operating instructions are issued centrally, telling the assembly-line workers that new, more efficient methods have been discovered and should be implemented – 'synthetic phonics' or the 'three part lesson', for example.

The work-force itself cannot be entirely trusted to be effective and responsible, so every so often external, national forms of quality control are imposed, and teams of inspectors visit the production line to make sure everything is being carried out as ordered. If not, the teacher-technicians are told to pull their socks up, and in the last resort the management can be sacked and replaced. Though many of the operatives see themselves and their students in quite different terms to these – as gardeners tending growing plants, for example – the deep embedding of the production line model in every facet of school life continually works against such competing metaphors.

As in the factory, the teacher-workers are supposed to be polite, punctual, meticulous, and respectful of authority – and these qualities are also expected to be cultivated in the student-products. As they get nearer the end of the process, the students are encouraged to think, within reason, about what they are learning. Those who attend grammar school factories are allowed to think about what they were doing a bit more than those whose basic mental material is presumed to be of lower quality, and who were sorted out and sent to less prestigious factories. Quality control requires considerable numbers of students to be graded as 'seconds' or 'rejects', but recently it has been thought that the workers shouldn't use that language for fear of damaging students' 'self-esteem', so confusing forms of language have been developed that mask the continuing quality control operation. Around half of all the products are regularly rejected after ten years of educational processing.

A slightly different version of the assembly-line metaphor describes the teachers as 'managers' and the students as 'workers'. The classroom is a 'work-place' where students do 'work' which they sometimes have to continue or elaborate as 'home-work'. They are told to 'get on with their work' and asked how their 'work' is coming on. As in a factory, work involves the completion of a task or the creation of a product that passes 'quality control'. If you continually produce such work you are a 'good worker'.

In this analogy, the point is not to think about what you are doing, or to develop any particular ability or understanding from doing it; *the point is to get the job done and complete the work satisfactorily.* Getting the job done to avoid being kept in after school is as valid as getting it done because you are interested in it. The fact that 'work' often equates to 'drudgery', and the opposite of 'work' is 'play', is not significant in this model. What matters is the product. The teacher's job is not to help student-workers think or learn; it is to assign tasks and manage the process so the work gets done properly and smoothly. They keep order, issue permission to leave the work-bench for trips to the toilet, scold or encourage the less efficient or the less motivated, and dispense rewards and punishments.[64]

Upholding the status quo

There are those who still think that the only kinds of educational reform we need are those that reaffirm these images. They are members of the counter-reformation: those who think that all we have to do is turn the clock back to the Good Old Days when we taught Latin and leadership to the bright young people who were going on to run

Parliament, the army and the Church, and needlework and diligence, sums and obedience, to the rest.

We have already seen a number of reasons why this nostalgic vision of education will not do. Of its 'successes', as many became confirmed in arrogance and dogmatism as developed the habits of open-mindedness and empathy. To the extent that Latin was ever associated with the development of powerful, useful mental habits, it was only because the study of Latin sometimes took place within a culture of educated discussion. It was the company of thoughtful and articulate people – if you were lucky enough to have it – that cultivated the educated mind, not the laborious translation of Roman poetry. Of the 'failures' of this bipartite system, a good many were left with a loathing of education, an almost complete ignorance of science, and a diminished sense of their own mental capacity. Human potential and resources were squandered. That has never been an acceptable cost.

Harking back to the abstract disciplined study of the grammar schools is no solution to the current problems and prospects facing young people. Behind the traditionalists' affection for the monastery and the factory lie inaccurate assumptions about many things: children's minds, the nature of 'ability' or 'intelligence', the nature of 'knowledge' and the relationship between intellectual comprehension and the development of expertise, amongst others. They believed that 'education' was a timeless process, divorced from the real stresses and opportunities of daily life, and that most young people lacked the mental equipment to benefit fully from it. They believed that somehow the quality of the minds that wrote Othello and invented calculus would rub off on those who studied the play and solved the equations. They believed that 'school' was a kind of magical place where studying difficult things prepared you for anything. They believed that well-informed reasoning paved the way for moral and intelligent action. In all these beliefs they were and are quite wrong.

The metaphor of apprenticeship

Whilst the two images of education as monastery and factory continue to provide a subconscious underpinning to our thinking about education, reforms are constrained. We can tinker with the curriculum – what needs to be 'added' to make an educated mind – and the examinations – the procedures for quality control – but the critical assumptions about what teaching and learning are, and what they are for, remain in place. Attempts to make education more interesting, topical and participatory often strain against these tacit strictures, but fail to break their hold. That is the main reason why educational reform so often goes round in circles. Real progress will depend on replacing the monastery and the production line with other, more compelling metaphors that open up new avenues of thinking.

The image of education as 'epistemic apprenticeship' that I mentioned in the preface is one such alternative. The idea of learning as an apprenticeship is even older than the monastery and the factory. In simpler and more stable societies, daily life itself was the classroom, the adults and older children going about their business were the teachers. They acted as informal guides and role models for the younger children, who observed, imitated and took small but increasingly responsible parts in the running of things. Through this unsystematic – but highly effective – process of osmosis, children learned not only the relevant skills, but also the values and beliefs of their culture, as they were enacted and modelled by those around them.

The factory and monastery models naturally draw our attention to the subject-matter of learning, and to the teachers' role in transmitting and explaining this knowledge, and in certifying that it has been passed on accurately. But the idea of apprenticeship balances this by focusing on the development of useful skills and qualities, and on the role of the teacher as guide and model rather than explainer and judge. In the school of the twenty-first century those skills and qualities are not specific, like hunting or weaving; they are the higher-order habits of mind that characterise the expert investigator, researcher, thinker and learner.

In developing the image of school as an epistemic apprenticeship, we have a new and powerful ally: the emerging sciences of the mind and brain (and not the science-lite of brain-friendly learning, but the real thing). For 4,000 years schools have been built on rather simple understandings of how brains and minds work. In the last thirty years, those understandings have been radically overhauled, and in some ways overturned. As our knowledge about the mind has changed, so it has opened up new questions, and new possibilities, within the field of education.

4

The intelligent child: old beliefs and new science

It is increasingly evident that the educational methods we have been using for the past 70 years no longer suffice. They are based on scientific assumptions about the nature of knowledge, the learning process, and differential aptitudes for learning that have been eclipsed by new discoveries.

Professor Lauren Resnick[65]

Zumbac the tailor had an unrivalled reputation. It was said he could make clothes to fit anyone. So my grandfather went, was extensively measured, and ordered his suit. A week later he collected it and tried it on. He took it back to Zumbac and complained that the left sleeve was a little longer than the right. 'Not a problem,' said Zumbac, 'just lift your right shoulder up a little.' My grandfather did as he was asked, and sure enough, the two cuffs were now the same length. But a few days later he went back again and said the right trouser leg was a little short. 'Don't worry,' said Zumbac, 'just bend your left leg a little and I think you'll find it fits.' Sure enough, the two trouser legs now matched perfectly. A third time he went back. 'It's too loose over the shoulders,' he said, 'the cloth wrinkles up.' 'Easy,' said Zumbac, 'hunch your shoulders forward a little and push your chin out.' And sure enough, the cloth stretched and flattened out and there was not a wrinkle in sight. As Grandfather was on his way home, he passed a man in the street who said, 'Don't tell me. You got that suit from Zumbac.' 'So I did,' said Grandfather, 'how can you tell?' 'He's an amazing tailor,' said the man. 'Only Zumbac could possibly make such a perfect suit for a man with as many deformities as yourself.'[66]

When school is seen in terms of the superannuated images we explored in the last chapter, it begins to look like one of Zumbac's suits. Once one of these images takes invisible hold, then a good many perfectly healthy children (and teachers) have to contort themselves to meet its demands. For some, that is easy. For others, it is well-nigh impossible.

For example, if the rigid, regular structure of the traditional timetable is seen as somehow 'natural', then it follows that children's minds have to be capable of switching subjects on demand. If the retention and manipulation of abstract knowledge, remote from one's own experiences and concerns, is what is required, then to prosper, minds must be able to divorce themselves from the immediate and the practical. Minds that can do these things are deemed to be 'quick' and 'bright'. Children who are upset by abrupt changes of topic, or unready to deal with abstractions, either have to try to hunch their minds up to fit, or risk becoming seen as 'difficult' or 'dull'. Intelligence becomes defined as the kind of mind that responds most readily to the peculiar demands of school.

Once you become an insider, a native of this educational world, then many ways of thinking about children's minds, their capacities, their intelligence and their development seem absolutely necessary and simple commonsense. But if you step outside, and look at learning and the nature of the mind from a different angle – especially if you do that with the help of a little contemporary cognitive science – then things appear very different. The metaphors of school as monastery and factory embody psychological assumptions that were uncontested at the time when modern schools were being designed in the nineteenth century. But they do not fit well with what we now know about children's minds, nor with the kinds of epistemic mentalities and identities that young people now need.

Intelligence: from fixed to learnable

Scientists' understanding of 'intelligence' has changed significantly over the last twenty years. From the late nineteenth through most of the twentieth century, a particular view of intelligence held sway in psychology. In the early decades of the twentieth century this view seeped out into the world at large – and especially the educational world – so that it came to be seen as 'natural' and 'normal'. This view influenced a great deal of educational thinking, and still does. Here are some of its hallmarks:

Intelligence was seen as a *unitary* quality of mind, distinct from other faculties like 'memory' or 'perception' – and certainly different from 'personality'. Being 'curious' or 'tenacious' were not the same kinds of things as being 'smart'.

Intelligence was seen as *general-purpose*, a kind of central reservoir of non-specific mental competence that determined how you would go about a wide range of things. If you were 'bright', your brightness would go with you into your history lesson, your workplace, your family meal-time, even into your athletics training. You were not just 'good at sums'; you were a 'bright child' or a person of 'average ability'.

This kind of intelligence was thought to be relatively *fixed*. People's 'ability' was a stable feature of their minds that not only didn't change much from place to place or activity to activity, but also stayed much the same over time. Being 'dim' stayed with you, in the same way that your eye colour or your blood group stayed with you. Many people thought that intelligence, like eye colour and blood type, was determined genetically. 'Nature' counted for much more, in the ability stakes, than 'nurture'. This emphasis on fixity led many people in education to focus more on what could not be changed about a young person's mind, than on what could.

The very core of this model of intelligence was *rationality*. Though your brightness affected many things you did, it manifested most importantly in conscious, explicit, deliberate, logical thinking. Such thinking was seen as of overwhelming importance in life, as in school. The better you were at this kind of thinking, and the more you used it, the better off you would be. Deliberation was generally the most powerful kind of thinking to use. And this kind of thinking was revealed in clear, logical speech and, most importantly, in writing.

A corollary of this view was the idea that your performance at solving abstract logical puzzles, devoid of context, personal relevance or experience – especially if you could do it fast and under pressure – was a good indicator of how much 'intelligence' you had. So-called 'IQ tests' composed of such puzzles could be used as an easy, valid and reliable kind of dipstick to indicate how deep someone's sump of general-purpose ability was. So people differed in the *amount* or level of 'intelligence' they had, and this was a very important thing to know about them.

Someone's level of 'intelligence' indicated what they could be expected to achieve: what the upper limit to their 'potential' might be. One of the most useful things that someone's level of intelligence predicted was their ability to learn. Bright people learned faster, more easily and more effectively than average or 'dim' people. They didn't make mistakes: they got things right, first time. Thus, when someone was finding learning hard, or they were making mistakes, that could often be interpreted as showing that they were getting close to the limit of their 'intelligence'. Young people who struggled more, or more often, with their school learning were usually – unless there was some obvious other reason – not as 'bright' as those who struggled less.

As I said, this view of intelligence has had a major influence on the British education system. For example it was used to justify the introduction of the eleven-plus exam that funnelled children into different kinds of education on the basis of their presumed 'intelligence'. The Spens Report of 1938 declared that:

> Intellectual development during childhood appears to progress as if it were governed by a single central factor, usually known as 'general intelligence' . . . It is possible at a very early age to predict with accuracy the ultimate level of a child's intellectual powers . . . It is accordingly evident that different types of children, if justice is to be done to their varying capacities, require types of education varying in certain important respects.[67]

Outsmarting IQ

This general view of intelligence may sound perfectly obvious to many people, but it has been challenged and modified by cognitive scientists a good deal over the last twenty years. The debate about the degree to which intelligence is inherited or acquired has turned out to be rather a waste of time. Even if there are – as there do seem to be – genetic differences in people's 'intelligence', there is, for everyone, a wide envelope of variation around that 'base point' that depends on experience, encouragement and self-belief.[68]

Imagine that the genetic component of 'intelligence' is like the size of a kitchen cooker. Someone may have three cooking rings and a single oven, and someone else has four rings and two ovens. These will set different hypothetical limits on the meals they can produce. But in practice, the quality and variety of their food generally reflects quite different things: how interested they are in cooking; the recipe books they have; how adventurous they are; who they can call for advice when a sauce curdles; and so on. In practice, neither of the cooks with the different sized cookers is anywhere near the limit of their cooking 'potential'. Any differences in their meals are much more likely to reflect differences in interest, experience and support than they do the addition of another burner or a fan-assisted oven.

Thus, scientists' interest has swung from trying to answer rather sterile questions about the absolute size of people's mental capacity to the exploration of how malleable and multifarious their mental habits and attitudes are. Although brains are, of course, not made of 'muscle tissue', but of intricate webs of neurons, it is now much more common for scientists such as Stanford University's Professor Carol Dweck to suggest that 'the brain is like a muscle' in order to explain the idea that minds are capable not just of being filled, but of being expanded. So it is not only more accurate, but also more profitable – and, indeed, more interesting – to look for ways in which every young person's mind can be stretched and strengthened, rather than to label them in terms of a hypothetical amount of 'brain power' that will not change.[69]

Many academic authorities have revived, and are quoting with approval, the great Swiss psychologist Jean Piaget's definition of intelligence. He thought of intelligence as 'knowing what to do when you don't know what to do'. In other words, the essence of intelligence isn't what you can do easily and fast. It is how you respond when the going gets tough. Do you have strategies and capabilities you can fall back on

– or do you go to pieces, like those 'bright' students in their maths test that we met in chapter 2? Being resilient and resourceful in the face of difficulty seems to be a much more useful kind of intelligence than being adept at solving logical puzzles and having a high IQ. Indeed, a recent study by Angela Duckworth and Martin Seligman of the University of Pennsylvania has found that young people's ability to stay focused and engaged with a difficult task and not give up, predicted their performance on school tests twice as well as did their IQ. 'Self-discipline' also predicted which students would improve their grades over the course of the next school year, while IQ did not.[70]

As resilience and resourcefulness are qualities that can be cultivated, it follows that people can be helped to 'get smarter'. The University of Pittsburgh's Professor Lauren Resnick is the doyenne of intelligence researchers in the USA. She suggests, in an article called 'Making America Smarter' that:

> Intelligence is the habit of persistently trying to understand things and make them function better. Intelligence is working to figure things out, varying strategies until a workable solution is found. Intelligence is knowing what one does (and doesn't) know, seeking information and organising that information so that it makes sense and can be remembered. In short, *one's intelligence is the sum of one's habits of mind*.[71](emphasis added)

Her research shows that this kind of intelligence is indeed learnable – and therefore teachable. Harvard's Professor David Perkins, another significant figure in the 'learnable intelligence' world, has concluded that short-term interventions are not useful and 'tend to enhance testmanship more than general cognitive efficacy, and yield effects that dwindle and vanish'.[72] However, more sustained changes to the way teachers work *do* have significant and lasting effects on students' everyday ways of thinking and learning so that they become second nature. Resnick explains:

> Students who, over an extended period of time are treated as if they are intelligent [in this sense], actually become so. If they are taught demanding content, and are expected to explain and

find connections as well as memorize and repeat, they learn more and learn more quickly. They [come to] think of themselves as learners. They are able to bounce back in the face of short-term failures.

It turns out that the key that unlocks the expansion of young people's intelligence is in the phrase 'they come to think of themselves as learners'. *The really important issue is not so much whether intelligence is innate or acquired, as what effect believing these different views has on the practical intelligence of the believer.* What researchers like Lauren Resnick and Carol Dweck have found is that these beliefs are powerful self-fulfilling prophecies. The belief in fixed intelligence has a direct and deleterious effect on the way that young people live their lives – and especially on how they go about learning.

For example, being labelled 'not bright' leads many young people to decide not to try to solve problems that they feel are difficult. Why waste the effort, if you've already accepted that you don't have what it takes? So, to put it crudely, believing you are thick makes it smart to not try too hard. What is not so obvious is that young people who come to think of themselves as 'clever' suffer just as much as those who have been labelled 'average' or 'weak'. It is not the specific ability level that has been attributed to you that does the damage; it is the belief that having to struggle suggests that you've reached the limits of your ability. A*ny* ability label, if you believe it to be valid and fixed, has the effect of weakening commitment and effort in the face of difficulty.

'Bright' students may struggle less often, but when they do, they are even more prone to feeling stupid that their 'less able' peers. Students who have been told they are 'bright' often come to associate their brightness with easy success. If they find themselves unable to do something easily, and having to try harder, that feels to them like evidence that they are not as bright as they are supposed to be. They are not living up to their billing. That is an uncomfortable thing to feel – so 'trying' itself becomes aversive. It turns out that 'bright' girls are especially prone to go to pieces when confronted by something they don't immediately know how to do. Indeed, many successful people are badly thrown by their first experience of real failure, whenever it comes. It's not just that they didn't get the result they wanted or expected; they may also suffer a full-blown identity crisis.[73]

Self-esteem

At the risk of labouring the point: it is not finding things hard or confusing that is the problem. It is the automatic, barely-noticed thought process which converts difficulty and mistakes into a self-critical judgement of inferiority. When students don't see that it is the *interpretation*, not the fact, of failure that is affecting their feelings, their determination to learn is always going to be brittle.

When teachers don't make this distinction, they can get themselves into all kinds of tangles trying to hide failure from the students, and remove difficulty from learning to avoid damaging students' self-esteem. This muddle about self-esteem is one of the main drivers of 'dumbing down'. When students and teachers accept the fixed-ability view, and its corollary, that failure undermines self-esteem, it is not surprising that teachers pull their critical punches, necessary feedback is not given (or acted on), and standards drift downwards. Students gain As at A-level, but can't write decent essays? Well, it's not surprising, if they have never been challenged, for fear of making them (or their parents) angry or upset.

In an attempt to shore up self-esteem, some teachers have tried to create an upwards glide-path of learning that is so shallow that nobody ever struggles. This is well-intentioned but misguided, for two reasons. First, nobody ever got more robust at learning by avoiding difficulty (just as nobody ever got fitter by avoiding exercise). The research shows it is the students who are most protected from the rigours and frustrations of learning that are the most vulnerable and brittle when they finally meet it. Second, challenge is exactly what students want. Easy stuff is boring. So watering down the curriculum in an effort to stop anyone ever getting upset is completely the wrong thing to do. It's that pernicious fixed-ability belief that is the fly in the ointment; not difficulty or frustration per se. Real self-esteem comes from the satisfaction of having managed to overcome difficulties to achieve something worthwhile. It is the *result* of a good bit of learning; not a necessary *precondition* for it.

A recent thorough review of all the research on the relationship between self-esteem and school performance has been carried out by Roy Baumeister and colleagues in the USA and Canada. They found, first, that the correlations between self-esteem and performance are actually very small. They account for only around 5% of the variability between students. Secondly, they found that deliberate attempts to boost self-esteem have no positive effect on performance, and sometimes actually make it even worse. They explain: 'An intervention that encourages students to feel good about themselves regardless of work [i.e. when the 'boost' is not linked to having done something well] may remove the reason to work hard – resulting in poorer performance.' Finally, they found that where there *is* a positive correlation between self-esteem and achievement, this reflects students' feeling good *because* they have done well, and not the other way round. (They also found, by the way, that people with high levels of self-reported self-esteem were often deluded, conceited and narcissistic! Many aggressive young men turn out to have a high – but brittle – sense of self-esteem).[74]

Journalist Melanie Phillips in her book *All Must Have Prizes* rightly ridicules these contortions. She says, witheringly:

> At some point in the last few decades, the educational world came to agree that its overriding priority was to make children feel good about themselves. None of them should feel inferior to anyone else or a failure . . . Nothing was to be difficult, everything in the education garden was to be fun. The uncomfortable truth that little of value is achieved without effort, in education as elsewhere, was decried as a form of child abuse.[75]

As we have seen it is not only students who are doing badly in school for whom the fixed-ability view is a problem, it also affects those who are succeeding, and impacts on older students like undergraduates. A 2006 study found that the belief that ability is fixed undermines people's confidence even if they keep succeeding. Women undergraduates who agreed with the statement that 'ability is a fixed attribute that cannot be developed over time' were more likely to suffer from 'imposter syndrome'. This is the belief that your success is somehow fraudulent, and that you are at constant risk of being unmasked as less 'bright' than you have 'fooled them' into thinking you are. One of the costs of this misconception is that you keep having to prove yourself. Believers in fixed ability are more anxious and competitive. They have to keep reassuring themselves that they are genuinely bright by being better than the rest. And that means they enjoy learning less for its own sake. They tend to disagree with the statement: 'I do my work because I like to learn new things.'[76]

Getting smarter

What happens to your learning if you ditch the belief in fixed ability? If you believe that 'it is possible to get smarter', you see your mind as an expandable collection of skills and habits. Effort takes on quite a different meaning: it is the pleasurable stretch that you feel when you are expanding your mind. Having to try means giving your mental muscles a workout. So, not surprisingly, people who believe in expandable minds try harder, find trying more enjoyable, enjoy learning more for its own sake, and are much more interested in 'learning how to learn' – for the very simple reason that their belief system can entertain that as a real possibility. They are also more ingenious, and more thoughtful about how they are learning. They like challenges that enable them to hone and develop their mental resources, and are more inclined to seek such challenges. It's the difference between constantly feeling you have to *prove* yourself, and feeling free to *improve* yourself.[77]

If education is to focus on developing useful capacities to cope with real-life problems and uncertainties, then we must discard the belief that minds come with a predetermined and immutable capacity. Yet it is an idea that seems amazingly resilient in the face of all the evidence. If the idea of expandable intelligence, and of education as helping that expansion to happen, is scientifically credible, educationally practical, and socially desirable, why does the old idea seem to have so much control over people's minds? The fixity focus seems to be a very successful example of what scientists Richard Dawkins and Susan

Blackmore call a 'meme': a tenacious, self-replicating idea.[78] It has colonised the minds, the tongues and the pens of Anglo-American educators for almost a century, and shows little sign of giving way. Current literature from the Department for Children, Schools and Families is still saturated with encouragement for teachers to attribute levels of 'ability' to their students and teach them accordingly.

Why is the idea of fixed intelligence so resilient and robust? I think there are three reasons, one economic, one psychological and one to do with teachers' lives.

The economic reason is that the fixed view of the mind provided a solution to the perennial question of how to allocate scarce and expensive educational resources. The further along the educational conveyer belt pupils go, the more expensive their teaching-and-learning operations become; and funds are limited. And, as Plato said, societies need a lot more followers than leaders. So a weeding-out process has to be designed that will identify those who will benefit most from higher levels of education: that is, those for whom the Return on Investment (ROI) will be high. Ordinary tests of achievement are one possible answer, but there is an obvious problem. An assessment of 'learning so far' is not always a fair indication of a young person's capacity to benefit from further study. Many good performers go on to 'underachieve' for a range of reasons: they are preoccupied for a while by being bullied or by anxieties about family members; they are demoralised by a particular teacher, but are perfectly able to recover later on; and so on.

What is needed, to maximise the ROI, is a prediction of their 'ability' to benefit from further years of education. Hence IQ testing and the eleven-plus examination. And hence also the powerful tendency of teachers, especially in the UK and the USA, to attribute to students a level of 'ability' that would enable them to make those predictions. 'Kyle's had a spot of bother, but he's a bright lad. He'll go far.' Or: 'Emma did very well in her maths, but I think she's just about reached her limit.'

The psychological reason for clinging to 'ability' has to do with the general human tendency to attribute stable characteristics to other people on the basis of inadequate information. We see someone behave once or twice in a particular way, and infer that they are 'mean-spirited' or 'irritable' or 'self-centred' or whatever. But when we look at ourselves, we take the situation into account much more. You yawned because you are insensitive. I yawned because I was tired. You are a bully. My anger was justifiably provoked. In our desire to find other people predictable, we underestimate how variable they are. This tendency is so ubiquitous that psychologists have given it its own name: they call it the Fundamental Attribution Error.[79]

The third reason has to do with the enormous complexity of teachers' lives, which renders them even more susceptible to this kind of labelling than the rest of us. It is a matter of sheer self-preservation. Five or six times a day, secondary school teachers find themselves in one of the most complicated social situations imaginable: a classroom of thirty or more young people, each of them a unique, complicated adolescent, and many of them working very hard on further developing their individual personas. Every teacher's day involves encounters with 150 or more such students. What could be more understandable than the need to impose some sort of order on this seething mass of personalities and interactions; to find a lens through which all this richness can be reduced to a manageable number of salient characteristics? 'Jason's a little terror.' 'Kelly's easily upset.' And ability attributions help enormously. Jason is not only troublesome but 'very bright'. Kelly is 'weak' as well as emotionally fragile. And David's helpful, and quite average.

These attributions of 'ability' are sometimes made on the basis of special questionnaires (like IQ tests), but often, in practice, they reflect teachers' observations of and inferences from students' classroom behaviour and levels of performance. Of particular importance are their achievements in high status subjects, especially English and maths, maybe assessed over quite short periods. These are often coupled with impressions of children as being quick (or slow) on the uptake, and generally obliging (or bolshy). Such judgements, once made, are hardly ever rescinded. It is as rare for a 'bright' child to be recategorised on the basis of a run of poor results, as it is for a 'weak' child to be upgraded if she goes on to do well. The bright child will be described as 'not fulfilling their potential', and some ancillary explanation found – home circumstances or having got in with a bad crowd, for example. The 'over-achieving' weak student will probably be credited with a surge of effort, rather than an increase in 'ability'. These labels tend to be very sticky and hard to peel off once they have been applied.

Yet spurts and dips in school performance are the rule rather than the exception – for all of the reasons I have just alluded to. For example, *less than half of the children who came in the top 5% on the national tests at eleven go on to remain in the top 5% at GCSE.* Despite such statistics, the *Times Educational Supplement* of 3 March 2006 reported that the Specialist Schools and Academies Trust (SSAT) have drafted a plan, with the DfES, to encourage universities to establish links with the pre-teen students who excel in these year six tests. The Trust's chairman is convinced that 'bright eleven-year-olds' should achieve three As at A-level, and wants secondary school heads 'held accountable' if those students don't make it. The SSAT is going ahead to build up a register of the most 'gifted and talented' students, so they will not be 'let down' by their secondary schools.[80]

Those who get on the list may indeed benefit from the so-called 'Pygmalion effect', or self-fulfilling prophecy, whether their inclusion is justified or not. They may also suffer from the weight of expectation and pressure that being 'registered bright' places them under, and become more anxious and conservative learners as a result. Those who don't make it onto the list may, of course, suffer from a reverse Pygmalion effect, and stand less chance of pushing their way forward if they happen to be a late-developer. They might equally be relieved of the pressure, and live happier lives.

Beware 'giftedness' and 'potential'

We should be aware of recent attempts – in the face of all this research – to re-focus attention on fixed aspects of students' minds by changing the vocabulary. Calling some students 'gifted and talented', for example, is fine, if all you mean is that their current levels of performance (in football, maths, piano etc.) surpass those of their peers, and that they should be encouraged to continue. But if the phrase slides back into meaning 'possesses inherent, all-round, high ability', then it has to be rooted out. The label 'gifted' is actually an honorific bestowed on children who have already developed certain social and learning skills and attitudes, such as making eye contact, smiling and nodding, and asking questions derived from what has just been said. These habits of mind are learned by children lucky enough to have grown up in families where they are modelled and encouraged. There is no reason why they cannot be further cultivated in school, both by those who already have them, and those that don't.[81]

Or take the word 'potential', which is very popular at the moment, as in 'encouraging all students to fulfil their potential'. This is fine if such sentiments mean we should be careful not to underestimate how much anyone might surprise us in their future achievement or interests. But if the word 'potential' starts to be used to suggest that some children have 'greater potential' than others, then we should be concerned. When used this way, many fall into the trap of thinking that low-achieving students have less 'potential' than high-achieving ones. But you could equally reason the other way round. People who have not achieved a great deal yet have more room for improvement, and so 'more potential'.

It is also helpful to remember that a commitment to 'fulfilling your potential' is confusing and potentially exhausting. How do students know when they have fulfilled it? Or is it an endless exhortation to achievement? Whatever happened to putting your feet up and reading the paper, or to a nice leisurely stroll in the country (as opposed to an earnest power-walk to get fitter)? As Professor Erica McWilliam of Queensland University of Technology says, it is a fundamental human right to decline the invitation to 'fulfil your potential'.[82] And to resist the views of life (as striving) and of the mind (as fixed-capacity) that such an innocent-sounding word might be infected with.

The main point of all this discussion is simple: it doesn't really matter if some fraction of so-called 'ability' or 'intelligence' is fixed. What matters is that much of it isn't. That is the bit that it is healthy and interesting for young people and their teachers to focus on. What is crucial is the shift of attention from what might be immutable to what is definitely expandable. For, in reality, the human mind is enormously elastic. No one in school is operating anywhere near the ceiling of their 'ability'. If you are on the look-out for them, you need never run out of ways of getting smarter.

A richer view of intelligence

While fixity was the mainstay of the old view of intelligence, there were, you recall, a number of other features that went along with it, some of which have also come under scrutiny in the preceding discussion. Intelligence is not immutable, but it is clearly not insulated from personality either. Being smart is as much a matter of determination and self-discipline as it is of intellect. And the way learning and achievement are influenced or 'capped' is much more to do with one's *beliefs* about ability than it is to do with any crude measure of ability itself.

Intelligence is not unitary: it is, as Lauren Resnick said, the sum total of one's habits of mind – and the relevant habits are many and various, and most of them can be cultivated. For example, thinking and acting intelligently involves many more facets of mind than the purely intellectual, rational, articulate ones. To deal with tricky real-life situations, you need to be able to attend carefully to experience and not leap to conclusions. You may need to take a different perspective on a situation, or put yourself in someone else's shoes. You may need to be able to take a step back and ask yourself if there is a different approach you might try, or if you are making any unnecessary or unhelpful assumptions. You may need to let your imagination loose and see what non-obvious possibilities it can come up with. Or you may need to sit quietly and mull the situation over, not chasing after a logical solution but being sensitive to any small intuitive promptings or inklings that may occur to you. All of these traits are at least as useful, in dealing with real-life difficulties, as being able to reason logically.

Once the old Procrustean definition of intelligence is put firmly in its place, quite a lot of accepted educational practice begins to get freed up. Teachers can let go of the easy tendency to interpret levels of achievement as evidence for differences in 'ability'. They can focus instead on the attitudes and habits of mind that are capable of being strengthened, and to look for the best ways of stretching and exercising them. They can wonder about how to cultivate resilience, intuition or empathy, as well as worrying about 'time management' and essay-structuring. They can concentrate more on helping young people build a broad, practical, working intelligence, and less on endlessly teaching them *about* things, at one remove, and incessantly analysing and explaining them.

Schools can begin to question the presumption that 'learning' is what young people do sitting behind a desk; that what they do elsewhere is not 'proper' learning, or not as valuable; and that 'teaching' is essentially about explaining things and setting exercises to ensure comprehension. And they can explore the possibility that it may not be necessary for so many young people to emerge from school as apparent failures. Perhaps there are different kinds of value that schools can add to young people's minds. Perhaps the traditional selection and quality control functions of school are themselves misconceived. Our imaginations are liberated to play with more possibilities.

5

Knowledge in the Google age

> If education is always to be conceived along the same antiquated
> lines of a mere transmission of knowledge, there is little to be hoped
> from it in the bettering of man's future.
>
> Maria Montessori

Zumbac's school forces children to fit a particular mould of learning, and values them according to how easily they can do so. But it is not just individuals who suffer at the hands of these Zumbacian images; it is the very conceptions of knowledge, of teaching, and of how schools should be organised and run that have to be bent to fit. If knowledge consists of timeless truths that can be written down, then dull text-books and dictated notes are obvious ways of transmitting them. If a fifty-minute lesson is somehow taken as the norm, then knowledge has to be capable of being cut up into ideas that will fit the available slots, and teaching becomes the design of activities that can be accommodated within such short spans of time.

Kinds of knowing that cannot be easily explained and sequenced by a teacher, or whose mastery cannot be easily demonstrated (on paper, under pressure) by children, are inconvenient in Zumbac's school, so tend to get marginalised or excluded. The most important, high-status subjects become those that are most amenable to this kind of Lego-like learning. In this chapter we shall expose some of the assumptions on which the Zumbacian views of knowledge, teaching and the curriculum are based, and – in most cases – discover that they need to be swapped for others that are more accurate, more productive, and better fitted to the times.

Knowledge: from precious commodity to 'what works'

When the first state schools were being designed in the nineteenth century, the curriculum consisted of the three Rs of reading, 'riting and 'rithmetic, and some other bodies of knowledge that any 'educated person' ought to know (or at least be familiar with). Because these bodies of knowledge were seen as reliable, timeless and of intrinsic worth, it wasn't anybody's job to ask where they came from, how they were made, who made them, whether there were any alternatives, if they were incomplete or whether they could be improved in any way. That wasn't the job of the teachers, and it certainly wasn't the job of the students. Drawing on the monastic metaphor, knowledge was seen as something that had either been handed down by unimpeachable Authority, or had been mined and purified, once upon a time, like gold, by men (mostly) who were very much cleverer than both the students and the teacher, usually in places called universities. Certain other cultural treasures also came to achieve this 'gold standard' status: the works of Shakespeare, Wordsworth, Beethoven, Constable and the like.

The teacher's job was to understand this knowledge (and these iconic cultural products) and explain them clearly. The students' job was to understand what they were told and remember it. They had done their job well if they could recall it, write it down, and manipulate it in a limited number of prescribed ways. They might have to 'derive an equation' or solve a stylised problem, or 'show how the poet achieves his effect', for example. Teachers were quite justified in speaking mostly in what you might call 'Is-language': this *is* the formula for copper sulphate; these *are* the most important rivers in Africa; 6 x 4 *is* 24; there *were* Three Wise Men; and so on. If students dared to ask questions (other than to correct their understanding) the Right Answer was repeated, and they were told they weren't there to 'reinvent the wheel', and anyway, there wasn't time. Once one of those clever individuals had got it 'right', there was no point in trying to argue about it. And it was quite presumptuous even to think you could.

Well, we all know that knowledge isn't like that *really*: it is always contentious and incomplete. For instance, people are still arguing about what Aristotle wrote, and what he meant by it. In this case, the problem is compounded by the fact that the lecture notes that survive show that Aristotle wasn't ever trying to explain a fully worked-out philosophy; he was always saying, 'Let's see what happens if we assume this,' or 'Let's look at it this way for a bit.'

Socrates was even worse. He'd say anything to try to get his students to think; to become aware of and challenge their own taken-for-granted beliefs. As students come with many different kinds of misconceptions, he had to say different things to challenge them (like a doctor writing different prescriptions for patients with different disorders). So it looks like he was continually contradicting himself – very confusing for the people who were trying to boil him down into a textbook chapter. Both Aristotle and Socrates saw 'knowledge' not as an end in itself, but as a resource for getting worthwhile things done – like persuading people to think for themselves. Their 'wisdom' was a stream of highly contingent, situation, problem and person-specific interventions and provocations; not nuggets of Truth.[83]

To take another example, the great physicist Neils Bohr came up with the 'mini solar system' model of atomic structure, and for many years it was taught to physics students (including me) as if it was The Truth. But in his autobiography, Bohr's friend and colleague Werner Heisenberg – he, appropriately enough, of the famous Uncertainty Principle – said that Bohr never believed that there really were little things called electrons whizzing round a tight little bunch of other things called protons and neutrons. It was an image – a pictorial device – he constructed to give his colleagues a very rough idea of how the mathematical equations worked to explain the observations. Heisenberg says: 'Bohr has formed an intuitive picture of different atoms; a picture he can only convey to other physicists *by such inadequate means* as electron orbits and quantum conditions. It is not at all certain that Bohr himself *believes* that electrons revolve inside the atom.' [Emphasis added.] And then, of course, a lot of other people came along and argued with Bohr, and dreamed up other ideas that might explain the observations even better, like 'quarks' and 'super-strings'.[84]

That's how knowledge is. Unless you are in the esoteric world of mathematical proofs and deductions (and possibly even then) , it is always provisional and always up for reappraisal. It is made up by people to explain puzzling things and to help get things done. Historical knowledge is there to stop us repeating the mistakes of the past. Grammatical knowledge is there to help people write better – that at least is the theory. If it works, great. If it doesn't then maybe we should look for something better. Shakespeare is wonderful but maybe he's not the best vehicle for developing the sensibilities of today's fourteen-year-olds. Once you focus clearly on the habits of mind that are being developed, and not on the retention of knowledge per se, it becomes an empirical question; not a matter of heresy.

And indeed, some of these questions have been put to the empirical test. In one recent experiment, two Greek psychologists checked to see if fifteen-year-olds' attitudes to 'knowledge' influenced how they went about learning Newton's Laws of Motion. Somewhat to their surprise, they found that the students who saw knowledge as a provisional, human construction, constantly open to question and change, showed a deeper and more accurate understanding of Newton than did their peers who believed that Science was Eternal Truth. They conclude, rather dryly, that 'if we are interested in designing effective learning environments, it is important to . . . develop curricula and instruction explicitly designed to promote epistemological sophistication'.[85] In other words, training students to think of knowledge as fixed makes them less smart – even when they are dealing with something as vener-able and time-worn as Newton's Laws.

Moderate relativism for the digital age

In the digital age, even more than in earlier times, knowledge is relative; it is 'what works'. Very rarely is there a block of 24 carat time-less wisdom, sitting on a nearby shelf, ready to solve your problem. In today's knowledge economies, the norm is for people to get together and make much of the 'knowledge' they need on the spot, in the context of the specific, complicated, not-quite-like-anything-else problem they are trying to tackle. There may well be some near-miss precedents that will help, but the necessary knowledge skills involve borrowing, customising, critiquing, combining and creating – not remembering and regurgitating. Being adept at gaining and using knowledge is what counts; not having a vast store of 'general knowledge', just in case. (It's better and easier to google it these days.)[86]

'Knowledge' is not what's true; it's what helps. Knowledge is what you use to get things done. It is situated and contingent. So we need people who are willing and able to critique, integrate, elaborate, challenge and work on and with the knowledge they come across. They need to see themselves less as nervous supplicants at the altar of knowledge, and more as confident critics and creators. And they need to be skilled at doing it well.[87]

Because knowledge is what helps people to get things done, the 'best' kind of knowledge depends on what the job is. There are arithmetical methods used by market traders and bookmakers, for example, that are very different from – and much more efficient than – the ones we were taught in school. They contain heuristics that are highly effective and elegant within their habitual domains. Abstract systems may be closer to Plato's world of pure 'ideal forms', uncorrupted by everyday experience; but for the kinds of mental calculation you need when making change in the market, rules of thumb work better.[88] If you want to explain the origins of the universe in a way that makes the most economical sense of a mass of detailed measurements and observations, you need to learn how astrophysicists think, and play by the sophisticated knowledge rules they have developed to guide their theory-building. But if you want to give your child a comforting sense of their place in a benign world, you might turn to Genesis. The Genesis myth does not begin to withstand the kind of scrutiny that the scientific cosmologist would apply; but equally, the scientist's story, for many people, fails to provide that sense of comfort and of belonging to a venerable tradition – and that purpose is just as valid as the urge to explain the scientific data.

There are a great many systems of belief and lore that look very superstitious to a Western scientific eye, but which work very well at regulating certain societies - perhaps even better than some of the more scientific and 'rational' systems. For example a belief in 'ancestor spirits' who can see into your mind can work very well at keeping people's anti-social impulses in check – what we try to do, often unsuccessfully, with ASBOs. It is when these knowledge stories try to compete for the same turf that things get confused. The failure to appreciate that different kinds of knowledge are fit for different kinds of purpose – just as maps are – lies at the heart of the sterile debate between evolutionists and creationists, for instance. We should be teaching young people to assess knowledge in terms of how well it does the job it was meant to do, not to create unnecessary antitheses.[89]

There is a sense, too, in which knowledge is becoming more democratic. It doesn't have to be carefully filtered and mediated by teachers and lecturers. There are many contemporary stories of geeky teenagers, unsuccessful at school, operating on the internet as legal or financial advisers, making good money and with satisfied customers. One fourteen-year-old boy in the USA set himself up as a share trader on the net and converted a stake of $8,000 into $800,000 in a year. Another fifteen-year-old's website offered highly rated advice on criminal law. He claimed never to have read a law book, and to have garnered much of his 'knowledge' from watching TV shows such as *Judge Judy*. These teenagers, functioning perfectly well in traditional professional roles, have simply by-passed the conventional educational routes, and 'cut to the chase'.[90] Of course there will be scams and failures in this more open epistemic world (just as spin in politics and sophistry in a court of law corrupt the world of 'pure reason'). But it is interesting that an experiment like Wikipedia, the internet 'encyclopaedia' where anyone can post and edit anything, seems to show that such radical democracy drifts over time, as people argue with and correct each other, towards greater consensus and a degree of organic reliability (though *caveat lector* is a good motto, and another good reason why we should be teaching young people to be sceptical, not reverent, consumers of knowledge).

If real-world, useful knowledge is a provisional, human construction, why on earth do we lead children to believe otherwise? Why do
we keep acting as if studying knowledge for its own sake, in a lacklus-
tre, reverential kind of way, is an important thing to do, without feeling the need to explain what such study is equipping them to *do* (other
than pass exams)? Why do schools trundle on, teaching past partici-
ples and the Vikings, as if oblivious to the fact that their students are
going to graduate into a knowledge-making world, not a knowledge-
applying one? Why do we not revel in showing them all the skills,
doubts, conversations and controversies that are the stuff of knowledge-making – and help them get better at doing these knowledge-
making things for themselves?

Plato's theory of education: the contagiousness of wisdom

Plato developed the 'timeless verities' view of the curriculum into a
complete philosophy of education: one which still casts a long shadow
over schools. His view was that through studying the best knowledge,
students' minds would become formatted along the same lines as the
great minds that produced it. And the more abstract and pure the
knowledge studied, the better it would develop and polish the students' powers of abstract reasoning – which Plato thought to be the
highest form of intelligence, and the one most needed in the future
leaders of society.[91]

As there could only be a few leaders, the subjects studied were also
designed to become more and more difficult and arcane, so most students would fail, or at least fail to stay the course (as the initial training
course for the SAS is designed to fail 90% of the applicants). Subjects
that were both formal and abstract – like mathematics and grammar –
were the best, because they were the least tainted by the ephemeral
details of mere experience, and especially by the corrupting influences
of emotion. Though they might dispute it, most schools today retain
more of Plato's abstract, intellectual philosophy than they ought. We
need schools that do something useful for the many, in the light of the
world as it is; not for the few, on the basis of some abstract, idealised
and questionable theory of leadership. The object of mass education

cannot be to sift out a few High Court Judges and Secretaries of State – nor, indeed, to breed professors of philosophy.

Further, there is clear evidence that mere contact with the products of great minds, or with elegant, abstract Platonic systems like algebra, does not make young people any smarter. A major study by Harvard's David Perkins has shown that, after primary school, there is almost no effect of education on how well people think in daily life, when they are outside their particular areas of specialism. When they are asked to think about a general social issue such as the effect of TV violence on people's behaviour, neither four years of secondary school, nor three years of undergraduate study, nor three years of graduate school, make any difference to the quality of their thinking. This is shocking, but it is true. Between the ages of eleven and sixteen, those 5,000 hours or so spent writing essays and drawing graphs produce virtually no improvement in the way young people think when they are outside the classroom or the examination hall. So if all that geometry (or those Latin translations) are not of much use in their own right, *and* they don't help you think better in real life, what exactly is the point?[92]

Interestingly, the old-fashioned teaching of grammar has been shown to be ineffective even in terms of developing pupils' practical literacy. A large-scale review of research carried out by academics at the University of York in 2005 found no evidence that teaching the parts of speech, noun phrases, relative clauses and so on helped five to sixteen-year-olds improve the quality of their writing. Predictably, the traditionalists retaliated to this attack on one of their most cherished beliefs by ignoring the research and reiterating their articles of faith. 'Children have to learn the basics of grammar and syntax before they can develop their writing,' thundered Nick Seaton, chairman of the 'Campaign for Real Education'. 'A knowledge of grammar must always come before creativity.' And blind faith and bombast must always come before a weighing of the evidence, apparently.[93]

To rub salt into the traditionalists' wound, another research study finds that teenagers' ability to 'know right from wrong' – to think and talk about moral principles and moral dilemmas – is unrelated to their propensity for antisocial behaviour. Intellectual study and discussion turns out to be an ineffective way of trying to get young people to behave better. On the contrary, old-fashioned teaching may well increase rebellious or disaffected attitudes – because it is youngsters' attitudes towards authority, such as teachers and the police, that predicts their bad behaviour, not their level of knowledge and ability to reason. Again, this finding jars so badly with the traditionalists' antiquated belief systems that they will almost certainly ignore it too.[94]

When you think about it, Plato's rationale doesn't even make sense. What students are doing as they grapple with the proof of Pythagoras's theorem or the theory of natural selection is entirely different from what Pythagoras and Darwin were doing when they were watching, wondering and deducing for the first time. They were indeed making knowledge, and hard, slow, creative work it was. They were using their powers of observation, deduction, imagination and reflection. The student is merely trying to understand and remember. They are using completely different sets of mental muscles. The 'contagion of excellence' argument simply doesn't add up. If the point of education really was to learn to think like Leonardo da Vinci, write like D. H. Lawrence, or see order in detail like Mendeleev or Darwin, students might be a lot more interested in school.

Simply studying these approved canons of knowledge and greatness does not help you learn to live your life. However, all is not lost, for it turns out that the *way* that you study them can make all the difference. It is the kind of learning you are practising that is important, not the subject-matter you are practising on. (Though, of course, as we shall see, different topics afford different kinds of practice.) That is why research shows that the specific teachers you have, and how they teach, matters a great deal more than the policies and procedures that a school adopts.[95]

Professor Jo Boaler of Sussex University has shown that the students in two classes can be learning exactly the same content, and even get more or less the same examination results – but one group can go away with a useful, general-purpose set of tools and attitudes that will stand them in good stead in their out-of-school lives, and the other doesn't. One student, with a grade B in GSCE maths, say, can take away an expanded mind and a greater sense of confidence and capability in tackling all kinds of real-life problems and difficulties, while another, with the same grade, has learned nothing of transportable value from the maths lessons at all. The first has been properly educated; the second has been merely schooled. The relative lack of attention to this third aspect of schooling – the 'epistemic apprenticeship' perspective – turns out to be one of the biggest failings of the status quo.[96]

The primacy of the intellect

Platonic ideas of education still influence which subjects are accorded pride of place in the school curriculum. Logical systems like algebra and grammar carry most weight. Those who are good at such subjects are defined as 'bright', and they have the most money spent on their education. If you can't do well at this kind of learning, diluted or less prestigious forms of education are made available.

But just for a moment suppose that we switched the rules of the game and made other kinds of intelligence, and different kinds of knowledge and expertise, the most prestigious, and offered the intellectual curriculum only to those who could not dribble a football or make mayonnaise. Imagine a society (of which there may well have already been many variants) in which physical education, design technology and art are the three most highly esteemed subjects, and English, maths and science are obviously less important because they only merit one lesson each a week, and they become optional when you are fourteen. The outstanding successes of the school are those who are strong, fit and physically agile; who can solve practical problems by inventing and building useful gadgets; and who can make elegant clay sculptures and take great photographs. This is the 'grammar school' curriculum, and to get into the school you have to pass the 'eleven-prac' exam, which assesses your ability to benefit from physical, design and artistic instruction.

If you fail, you go to a scruffy school down the road where you have to learn the parts of speech and do trigonometry and acids and bases. Children who are naturally bookish and enjoy writing are severely disadvantaged by the lack of fit between their strengths and interests, and those that the school clearly values. Professor David Hargreaves has tried to imagine how he might have responded to this 'nightmare scenario'.

I enjoy most lessons very little; I am bored and make little effort in areas where I seem destined to fail. The temptation to 'muck about' in lessons, and even to truant, is almost irresistible. My friends soon matter to me much more than anything else in school and our greatest pleasure is in trying to mock and subvert the institution we are forced to attend for five long years. I don't think my teachers, who seem so strong and clever with their hands and feet, really understand me at all. Quite often they are kind, but I know they look down on me and think it's all rather hopeless in my case. I'll be glad to leave school.[97]

The traditionalists, secure in their Cartesian world view, would find this scenario unthinkable – but I don't. I rather like the idea of an education that taught me to do something useful and practical, as well as how to talk and argue – though like David Hargreaves I would almost certainly have failed the 'eleven-prac'.

Is maths really so important?

You could argue that, beyond the obvious usefulness of basic arithmetic, mathematics has the status it does not because it is intrinsically important, but because it seems to fit the methods and assumptions of Zumbac's school so well. Mathematical knowledge is timeless. It can be easily segmented into topics. It can be clearly explained. Graded exercises can be constructed to guide practise. The steps of reasoning can be clearly set out so errors are easily spotted. There are unambiguously right answers, which make for rigorous and objective assessment. And, as a bonus, all you need to do most maths is paper and pen, so it is cheap and portable. The way real mathematicians actually solve problems and make discoveries is, of course, a million miles away from this clinical kind of learning.[98]

The Platonic assumption is that, because maths deals in ethereal entities like xs and ys, frictionless pulleys and perfect circles, that are unsullied by the nasty messy details of real experience, the learning that accrues should float free of specifics, and therefore be available to apply anywhere. But maths isn't 'no domain', it is a very special domain, and what is learned there is as tied to 'geometrical shapes', 'algebraic formulae' or 'written-out sums' as are 'cookery skills' to the kitchen. Mathematical domains are, at least to students, highly specific, if arcane, worlds akin to, but of more limited appeal than, those of Lewis Carroll, J. K. Rowling or Phillip Pullman. In a telling piece of research, my colleague Martin Hughes found that four-year-olds were perfectly happy to tell you that 'two plus three' equal 'five', and were even quite willing to say that 'two wuggles and three wuggles' make 'five wuggles', without having a clue what a wuggle was. But they refused to add 'two thousands and three thousands' because, they said, 'we haven't done thousands yet'. By four years of age they had already learned that maths was a very special and precarious world where you had to tread carefully, and had to wait to be 'taught' before you could move.[99]

The transfer problem

In the Platonic world, abstract knowledge comes to swim around in the mind, like goldfish in a bowl, waiting to be hooked by any relevant situation that might crop up. From this perspective, it may be hard to get something into your mind if it is difficult to understand, but once it is in, and you have understood it 'properly', then there is no problem, in principle, in fishing it out again when it is needed. It would be nice if this were true, but both the scientific research and everyday experience suggest otherwise.

We *can't* just assume that something learned in one context, for one purpose, will automatically come to mind wherever and whenever it might subsequently be useful. We all have times when something useful fails to 'come to mind' at the right moment. When I am doing the 'quick crossword', it may simply not occur to me that a four-letter synonym for 'shy' is 'hurl'; or the answer to 'sky' is 'loft'. The knowledge that 'shy' and 'sky' are words for different kinds of throwing or hitting actions – which I know perfectly well – just doesn't come to mind when it should: or not until I come back to the puzzle a few hours later, when I have remembered that the setter's art lies in precisely this kind of misdirection, and I deliberately start looking for obscure meanings.

There are a wealth of experiments showing how often 'transfer' of useful knowledge and skills from one setting to another fails to occur. Children who are trying to catch computerised butterflies, flitting about on the screen, with a stylised net, easily pick up the butterflies' habits and use this knowledge to anticipate their movements and set traps for them. But if you change the game to one in which the children are trying to predict where a geometrical shape will jump to, they can't do it, and they don't learn to predict the movements. It is exactly the same game, but change the superficial details and the children behave quite differently. 'Abilities' they seemed to have one minute have magically disappeared the next. In one context, the children are 'bright', you might say, while in the other they seem much 'dimmer'.[100]

Learning, as the cognitive scientists put it, is *situated*. What that means is, when you learn something, you do not automatically strip away all the incidental details of what exactly the task and the material were, and how you were feeling, and what time of day it was, to leave the 'essential learning' bare and exposed. On the contrary, these details form a normal part of the mental record of that learning experience. Knowledge and skills stay indexed according to when and how and why you learned it. So we should *expect* transfer – the generalisation of knowledge from one context to another – to be limited and fragile.

So we can't assume that 'transfer' will look after itself. If educators want useful things to become 'disembedded' in students' minds from their contexts of acquisition, so they will be called up and activated by a wider range of situations in the future, they have to work at it, deliberately and explicitly. Later in the book we shall see how this problem is overcome, but for the moment it is important to note that contrary to the Platonic view, learning is as much about knowing when and how to retrieve what you know as it is about registering and understanding it in the first place.

So the idea that a teacher can see a child do something, and then tick a box to say they 'possess' the relevant skill or ability is simply nonsense. You cannot observe that someone did something – solved a problem of one kind, in one context, for one purpose, on one day – and conclude that they will (or even should) be able to 'use it' on any relevant occasion in the future. You can't conclude 'does' from 'can'. Nor can you conclude from the fact that someone *didn't* 'communicate effectively' last Thursday in English that they aren't going to do so in maths today. You can't conclude 'can't' from 'didn't'. There are all kinds of possible reasons for 'didn't', like it just didn't come to mind, or they couldn't be bothered, or they were preoccupied. All of these would have to be exhaustively eliminated before you could conclude 'can't'.

This mistaken view of the mind has led people to think of school as a special kind of context-free zone – in rather the same way that people have thought of maths as a context-free subject – in which what is learned is devoid of personal packaging, and so able to be retained in a free-floating way. But 'school' isn't neutral, any more than 'mathematics' is. Just as maths is a particular, odd kind of world, so school is a very particular, odd kind of place, full of details, activities and purposes, many of which are quite unlike those that young people are going to find themselves operating in, once their formal education is over. School is not an 'off-the-job' experience, when normal indexing stops so that maximum generalisability can automatically occur. Being in school is very much 'on-the-job', full of peculiar tasks, settings and reasons. The problem is that the job you are on, in school, is not going to be very much like the jobs you will find yourself engaged in elsewhere (unless you are set on becoming a teacher or lecturer).

Far from being neutral, the oddness of school means that transfer is especially *unlikely* to happen. The apparent sudden forgetting of school knowledge (and the mental skills that went with it), after people have left, does not show that they didn't learn them 'properly' in the first place. It means that what they learned has stayed indexed to school-like conditions, and won't come to mind until those conditions are recreated. (You can prove this to yourself by doing a relaxation exercise and then taking an imaginary journey back to your primary school days. Recall the room, the teacher's face, the view from your desk, and you will be amazed at the wealth of forgotten detail that comes flooding back.)

In this chapter we have seen how an antiquated view of knowledge compounds the errors of dysfunctional views of the mind and intelligence. Yet to this day these superannuated assumptions still lurk behind the way we think about the curriculum, examinations and the activities of teaching and learning. Once we accept that knowledge is situated and 'for doing', not just for hoarding, and that minds are not just fillable but expandable, a whole new vista of educational possibility opens up.

6

Learning about learning

Education is what is left after you have forgotten everything you were taught at school.

Albert Einstein

Children are born loving learning, and they are born good at it. Actually, they start learning in the womb. For a foetus, learning might be attuning to the chemical signature of its mother's diet. For a baby, it might be learning to read its mother's mood from her face; for a toddler, learning to open a cupboard door; for a teenager, learning to apply make-up, to bend a penalty kick, or to make people laugh. Their learning agendas may not fit with ours, but if you look at them in the round, you will see young people are endlessly busy at learning.

Why learning is good for you

This innate learning appetite is highly intelligent, because learning is the gateway to everything. It is the portal that enables people to explore whatever they want to explore, and strive to become what they want to become. Learning makes it possible to earn a living, and to change careers - several times if needs be. Learning is the one capacity that you can be sure will never go out of date – unlike more specific skills such as programming your iPod. Specific kinds of skill and understanding come and go, but the need to be good at learning is perennial.

Learning makes people happy. The satisfaction of struggling with that crossword, and completing it; learning how to do the re-wiring yourself; getting the dog to sit; researching and booking the family holiday on the internet rather than taking the usual package: all these deliver, as pleasurable by-products, feelings of pride, satisfaction, competence and independence. The more of a learning life you lead, the more you are, and become, self-sufficient. Studies in 'positive psychology' show that taking on and making progress with your own challenges and projects is a more reliable source of happiness than winning the lottery. Getting what you think you want is consistently overrated as a source of happiness, and not getting it is overrated as a source of unhappiness.[101]

Learning makes people happy because it is inherently pleasurable. Psychologist Mihaly Csikszentmihalyi has found that learning – pushing yourself, taking on challenges – creates a feeling he calls 'flow'. Flow is a fancy name for being so engrossed, absorbed, rapt by something that time flies and you forget your worries. When your skills are being stretched (but not too much) by a ski run, a computer game or the intense effort to write a book chapter, you will report, afterwards, that you were happy. Successful students at school know the value of 'flow', and derive pleasure from the effort to 'get their heads round' a difficult idea.[102]

Learning enables you to see your life as a draft that can always be improved. Being an unapologetic learner means never having to pretend you're perfect. A learning attitude makes mistakes more tolerable and even sometimes interesting and useful. The more confident at learning you are, the more enjoyable life's challenges become and the better your self-esteem. If you are fearful of and intimidated by learning, you will have fewer choices in life and things will not go as well for you. [103]

Children are not 'unmotivated'

I am regularly asked: 'But what about the child who is completely "unmotivated"; who just doesn't want to learn anything?' My answer is that those children don't exist. There are kids who don't want to learn particular things, in particular settings, and there are those who don't find it easy to learn some things in some settings; but the generally lazy child who doesn't want to learn anything is a myth. What the questioner actually means is: 'They don't want to learn what I want them to learn, when I want them to learn it, in the way I want them to learn it.'

Many people seem to misunderstand the concept of 'motivation'. They think of it as an energising 'thing' that some kids just have more of than others. But 'motivation' is like 'ability' in being a composite term. It is a word for the resultant of a much more complicated set of interlocking processes and forces. When these line up one way, one kind of learning happens. When they line up differently, another kind happens.

If Jo looks 'unmotivated' to learn X, it can mean any combination of the following:

- Jo is not currently interested in X.
- Jo is interested in X but has competing priorities that are engaging her learning resources, often to do with emotions, self-doubt, family or friendships.
- Jo is tired or upset.
- There are distractions that are disrupting Jo's concentration, and/or Jo has difficulty concentrating.
- Jo is not confident in her learning; she doubts that her efforts and resources will be equal to the learning task.
- Jo doesn't like the person who wants her to learn X and wants to thwart him.
- Jo is frightened of what might happen to her at break-time.
- Jo believes that becoming good at X will conflict with her image of herself, or the values of her friendship group.
- Jo believes that if she tries and fails to learn X, she will feel even worse about herself than she does already, so it is better not to try.

For any or all of these reasons, or a dozen others, Jo can look to you like she is 'unmotivated'. Knowing all this does not undermine your right to get her to try to learn X – but it will increase your likelihood of being successful. The question is not whether young people can be per-suaded to learn. It is: what stops them, or puts them off learning.

How real-life learning differs from school learning

If the core purpose of education is to give young people a useful apprenticeship in the arts and crafts of real-life learning, then the kinds of learning they do in school – not the content, but the sorts of learn-ing activities which that content demands and exercises – has to match the kinds of learning that people do in the wider world. If education is to be a preparation for dealing with rich, messy, disconcerting life then it can't just train young people in how to hoover up pre-determined, bite-sized gobbets of knowledge.[104]

Here are some of the most obvious and generic differences between the way learning happens in school and the way it mostly happens in real life. Of course, as I have illustrated, real-life learning is incredibly multifarious. It covers everything from developing your dress sense to mastering a new frisbee throw, from writing more clearly to learning your times tables, from comforting a baby to chairing a good meeting. But we can make a few generalisations none the less:

- Real-life learning usually happens in the context of getting some-thing interesting done. Sometimes we browse a book or surf the internet just out of interest, but mostly learning is a means to an end, not an end in itself. Your learning was successful if you got where you wanted to go: pleased the people you wanted to please; passed your driving test; got the laugh; sold the painting; won the championship. In real-life you zoom in on a specific bit of focused learning at just the moment when you need it. Your learning is 'just in time', not 'just in case'. In school, a good deal of learning lacks that sense of timing. It is not opportune, in terms of the wider pro-ject you are pursuing. In school, learning, strangely, is made an end in itself, and the skills you are learning are to do with writing, explaining, discussing, critiquing – and passing exams.
- In school, learning is often piecemeal. It is broken down into little bits that you study one after another. Real-life learning rarely

comes ready-perforated and conveniently packaged like this. You are usually, gradually, getting better all round at what you are doing. You might be separately practising your dribbling, tackling and running-off-the-ball, but mostly you are playing football, and your speed, agility, ball control, tactical sense and general appreciation of the game are all developing together. You may play a 'junior version' of the full-blown game – five-a-side instead of eleven-a-side, say – but you are still, from the start, playing the whole game, not some cut-out bit of the game. When you are promoted to a new and challenging role in your company, your learning involves 'getting your head round' a whole lot of things at once, as you 'get a feel' for what the role involves, and progressively 'raise your game'.

- School learning usually involves solving problems of carefully graded difficulty. In real-life, there is nobody there to do the pre-grading for you, and the 'learning curve' you experience may be anything but smooth. Sometimes you make big strides, sometimes it is hard graft, sometimes you have insights, sometimes you don't seem to be getting anywhere at all. In real life, you respond to the vicissitudes in your own way, at your own speed. You usually have much more control over where, when, why and how you go about learning than you did in school.

- Real-life learning often involves a lot of collaboration and talking. Learning emerges out of discussion. A group of people may develop understanding and expertise together. No one knows 'the answer' ahead of time. No one person may have all of the pieces. More knowledgeable members of a team will help others to learn what they need to know. In school, though there is group work, learning is essentially individual, and eventually, come the test, may even be competitive. If the person at the next desk knows more than you, traditional education encourages you to see them as a rival, not as a resource. Collaboration is called 'cheating' or 'copying'.

Here are just a few of the learning techniques that people commonly use in real life:

- They watch how other people do things – run meetings, cope with confrontation, plant bulbs – and see if they can effectively copy what their role models are doing and adapt it to their own style.
- They go off by themselves, practise the 'hard parts', and then fit them back into the overall performance they are trying to improve – the speech, the innings, the recital.
- They ask their own questions, at the rate they need to, of the people they think can help best – they select their own 'teachers'.
- They make scruffy notes and diagrams to help them think and plan that no one is going to ever check or evaluate.
- They create half-baked ideas and possibilities, and maybe try them out on someone who they trust not to laugh at them.
- They run through things in their heads, imagining how different scenarios might play themselves out.
- They imagine themselves doing something better than they currently can, and then use that 'home movie' as a guide to help them practise.

In school, you may or may not make use of these kinds of general, powerful learning tools, but you will rarely hear them talked about, and often, as I say, the official tool-kit is narrower, more intellectual and more solitary.

In real-life learning, people may not talk about learning, or teaching, at all. They have a whole set of other ways to talk about learning. You are getting better at things, working on them, grappling with them, trying things out, doing tricky stuff, finding it hard, getting your head around something, pushing yourself, improving your personal best. In school, the vocabulary of learning is very different: instruction, objectives, curriculum, assessment, scheme of work and so on.

The wrong epistemic apprenticeship

So the epistemic apprenticeship currently offered by conventional schools exercises very different kinds of learning from those that will be most useful in real life. If what is called for in school is careful attention to a teacher, accurate retention of facts and ideas, and the ability to do certain kinds of stylised written exercises on demand, then we should not be surprised if young people complain that they are not being sufficiently readied for life. The missing key to effective educational reform is thinking how to narrow the gap between the way learning is 'done' in schools, and the way it is done in the outside world.

Learning real, difficult, meaningful things, in collaboration with others, with some responsibility for determining how they go about it: this is exactly what young people themselves say they want. The evidence from Cambridge professor Joan Rudduck and others is that, by the time they get to secondary school, if not well before, most of them are hungry for the three Rs – responsibility, respect and 'real' – and the three Cs – choice, challenge and collaboration:[105]

- They want to take *responsibility* for their learning.
- They want their views about their education to be treated with *respect*, to be listened to and taken seriously.
- They want *real things* to explore. That is, they want to work at things that have not been thoroughly worked over by thousands of people before, and preferably things that are of true value to somebody.
- They want *choice* in what, when, where and how they are learning. They would like to make some contribution to selecting the tasks and problems they are going to be working on, to have an understanding of what is required, when it has to be done by, what the marking criteria are – and then be left to get on with it, being supported, but not continually chivvied or supervised.
- They want the *challenge* of getting their teeth into difficult (but not demoralising) things, and experience of the satisfaction of making genuine progress.
- And they want *collaboration*. They want to be able to get together with other people and think and argue and struggle and learn together.

It is by meeting these legitimate, perceptive needs that we can help young people to develop the confidence that they crave.

How the brain learns

Let us back up for a moment and take a look at the science behind this kind of real-life learning, and the idea that it is possible to 'learn how to learn'. We can now improve considerably on the flawed view of learning and the mind that we critiqued in the previous two chapters. Neuroscientists and cognitive psychologists have much to say that can help us in our quest for a twenty-first century education system.

First, we need to remember the biological and evolutionary roots of learning, for without those roots there is nothing for the more sophisticated branches of adult learning to grow up and out from. Compared with all other animals, human beings are born in a highly immature and helpless state. This may be because, if they waited any longer, their heads would have grown too big for them to be born. For whatever reason, we arrive in the world very unfinished, and this is both good and bad news. The bad news is that we are therefore more vulnerable – we stay immature for longer – and need, as we grow up, care that is much more long-term and sophisticated than does a fledgling or a kitten. If the world we find ourselves in is not right, development has lots of opportunities to go wrong through accident, malnutrition or abuse.

The good news is that this protracted immaturity allows children to tune themselves much more precisely to the particular world in which they live. That tuning is what we call learning. Our brains are spectacularly sensitive to any patterns that recur around us that enable us to predict, and therefore control, what is going on. If a particular voice quality regularly heralds a drop in the quality of service a baby can expect from its mother, that is useful information. It can keep quiet till the voice perks up again. If the slam of a door is regularly followed by the appearance of a large male who seems pleased to see the baby, then the slam becomes a signal of a pleasurable encounter.

Most of these predictions are automatic. They get built into our reflex modus operandi by our brains, and we do not have to think about them – at least not all the time, and not when we are young. Our learning brains mould us to our surroundings, so that our chances of survival are increased, and we can pursue our interests, and avoid threats, more successfully, more of the time. The key is anticipation. If you can get those pupils dilated, those juices flowing, and that adrenaline pumping ahead of time, you will be in better shape to meet the upcoming world.

The first time you went on an escalator it probably felt funny. Your body did not know what to expect, and it could only clumsily adjust to the sudden acceleration. But after a few times, your brain figured out what fine adjustments to your balance were required, and linked those to the visual cues as you approached the escalator. You did not even have to break your stride or stop your conversation. Now, when you approach an escalator that is not working, despite the visual information in plain view, your brain sets up the same patterns of adjustment – and you stumble as you get on to the stationary stairway. Likewise, we manoeuvre our way down a busy street, scarcely aware of all the minute observations and adjustments we are making in order to avoid bumping in to people. Only occasionally do we get it wrong, and get locked into a cycle of mutual observations and adjustments with someone else that leads to a clumsy and embarrassing dance.

The fact that most of these predictions are statistical, not guaranteed, does not make them any less valuable. A baby anticipating its parents' return at the end of the day expects Mum or Dad to be in a good mood. Even a 70% chance of a good mood enables the baby to do two things – adjust to what is coming up, and even better, intervene to try to steer the anticipated course of events. So a cheerful gurgle might increase the likelihood of Mum or Dad stopping off to say Hello, and elicit a cuddle or a delightful game of Peek-a-boo. A baby's smile is not just a reflex response to feeling good; it is a social invitation to the recipient to feel good too – and thus to enter into a virtuous cycle of interaction.

Many things do not turn out as expected, and then more tuning has to take place. The brain learns by constantly monitoring how accurate its predictions turn out to be, and how effective the interventions which it generated were, and adjusting the neural pathways so that, next time, you will try something just a bit different. The brain is designed by natural selection for this endless round of prediction, monitoring and tinkering. That is the brilliant 'natural learning ability' with which we come bundled into this world. The brain continually distils the evanescent complexity of the world into ever more sophisticated maps of expectation and possibility. It is these maps that enable us to intervene more and more successfully in the flow of events.

The details of how brains learn are still being worked out by neuroscientists. Broadly, brains work in somewhat the same way that animals wear stable patterns of criss-cross tracks in a forest or a jungle. First you have to have a jungle: a mass of vegetation that can be altered by walking. The brain, after birth, generates an explosion of neural vegetation – 'exuberant growth', the scientists rather nicely call it – and then, out of all the potential connections that could be made, only those that are continually repeated survive. When A repeatedly occurs alongside or just before B, a groove is worn in the brain so that when A happens again, B automatically gets ready to join in. The groove allows the appearance of A to 'prime' B, so that you need less external evidence for B for it to 'fire'. As the neuroscientists sometimes put it, 'cells that glow together, grow together'.[106]

Emotion and learning

This wearing of neural grooves is heavily influenced by our own priorities: the portfolio of things that are significant to us: our desires, interests, worries and fears. Patterns that relate to these priorities recruit the brain's so-called 'limbic system', and its engagement ensures that those patterns get stamped in to the pathways of the brain more rapidly and more deeply than those of lesser importance. The most important events of all, the ones that arrest us and engage our more detailed attention, are those that both relate to our goals and also provide significant new information. A new signal for a cherished goal gets prioritised, as does a significant failure of a reasonably confident prediction. You thought it was just an ordinary mug of tea, and then, as you near the bottom, the head of a small frog breaks the surface. You pull the ears of the family dog, as you have hundreds of times before, and unaccountably she snarls and snaps at you. These are the learnings that make use of the neural systems that rely on the neurotransmitter dopamine, and which activate the deep arousal systems of the brain and get our attention.[107]

Neuroscience has required us to rethink our understanding of the relationship between learning and emotion. In the Platonic model of the mind (endorsed by Descartes and handed down to the nineteenth century founders of state education) emotions are mainly seen as a nuisance. Anxiety, frustration, even excitement are seen as potentially disruptive of learning. Emotions introduce subjectivity, and can distort the purity and trustworthiness of dispassionate reason. (One could argue that the curriculum has come to be dominated by dry, scholarly topics precisely in order to lessen the chances of any troublesome passions becoming inflamed, and perverting the course of true learning.)

This opposing of reason and emotion is, as neurologist Antonio Damasio called it in the title of his best selling book, Descartes' Error.[108] Damasio has shown that, without emotion and intuition, reason easily becomes detached from practical intelligence, and produces intellectually clever people who behave stupidly. From a functional point of view, emotions are general states of readiness to deal with broad kinds of threats and dilemmas. Fear is readiness to flee; anger is readiness to intimidate; sadness is readiness to withdraw and mourn; and 'interest' and 'intrigue' are the feelings that signal readiness to learn. Without some kind of emotional engagement, learning is slow and weak. Sportspeople know that much important learning has to happen within the emotional intensity of an important match. The skills of the practice pitch have to be tempered and honed in the heat of competition, or they may wilt on the day. Real mathematicians get incredibly passionate about the problems they are working on. Emotions weave through learning in ways that are much more intricate and positive than the old split allows.[109]

The intuitive brain

Our brilliant natural learning ability covers a broad spectrum from continual, small-scale, unconscious tuning and pruning, to dramatic moments of shock and disruption. At the less emotional end of the spectrum, all the brain needs, to do its job, is sensitivity to the information. You do not even have to be consciously aware of what you are learning, nor even that you are learning anything at all. This gradual development of intuitive expertise – 'getting the hang of it', as we say – is especially good for new, intricate practical situations. Relaxed 'trial and error', just playing with the situation without trying to consciously understand it, allows the brain to do what it is so good at: extracting the patterns that underscore the ability to predict and control. Absentmindedly messing about with things can lead to faster, more effective learning than careful thought. The brain is not designed for erudite displays of knowledge but for learning how to get things done quickly and fluidly in situations that matter. We are built for real-life practical learning, not for scholarship. Unless there is a good reason why you need to be able to explain what you are doing or what you have learned – sometimes there is, often there isn't – this kind of background 'learning by osmosis' is often the best bet.

In fact, scientists have shown that this kind of learning is often better if you are *not* consciously concentrating, or if you are not thinking about what you are doing. In one study, people had to interact with a console controlling an industrial process, and learn how to optimise the output of the computerised 'factory'. Open-minded trial and error turned out to be more effective than earnest attempts to figure out what was going on – especially when there were some variables at work that were counter-intuitive. If people had been given some prior experience with a random game, in which it became clear that there was nothing they could do to figure the situation out, they learned to control the factory process faster. The random game had effectively taught them to switch off the thinking part of their minds, and just let the brain learn from experience. Too much thinking can get in the way, and it is not intelligent to be 'clever' at the wrong time.[110]

The value of switching off thinking has also been demonstrated in more sophisticated kinds of learning and creative problem-solving, in which it helps to allow a more patient, dreamy kind of mental process to take place. There are many studies now that show that people who cannot access this state of reverie are less intelligent and less creative than those who can – especially when difficult, complicated decisions and judgements have to be made.

Ap Dijksterhuis of the University of Amsterdam has studied how people make such decisions, for example about which apartment out of a number of options to buy. There are a great many different considerations to be taken into account in making such a decision: size, price, state of repair, decoration, the garden, the neighbourhood, proximity to shops and public transport and so on. Dijksterhuis fed people a lot of bits of information about the different flats, and then asked them to pick the one they thought was overall the best buy. Some people were asked to make their decision immediately, while others had a few minutes' delay before they had to make their choice. Half of this latter group were encouraged to consciously weigh up the pros and cons of the different flats, while the other half were prevented from explicitly thinking about the problem by a secondary distractor task.

Astonishingly, of the three groups, it was the last one – the group who had a delay but were unable to think deliberately – that made the best use of the information they had been given. They were the most 'intelligent'. Dijksterhuis identified two factors at work here. First, when there are too many dimensions for conscious thought to deal with, the intuitive brain is better than the conscious, rational mind at keeping track of the incoming information, and integrating it into an evolving picture of the situation. And second, allowing time for the information to incubate in the back of your mind is helpful – more helpful, again, than the attempt to be explicit and methodical.[111]

Intuitions are now seen by cognitive scientists as physical and imaginative intimations of perfectly valid cognitive processes. It has been suggested that 'intuition' functions like a 'You've got mail' icon that blinks in the corner of the screen of consciousness. It signals a change in something behind the scenes, that you can 'click on' and bring up into consciousness later – like that nagging feeling in the corner of your mind that there is something you meant to do.[112] Being 'touched' or 'moved' by a film or a painting, but not being able to say why: these are valid and intelligent 'ways of knowing'. In school, though, the fact that such feelings and intuitions are hard to 'teach' and to assess means that they are lopped off: simply removed from the operative definition of intelligence. But in doing this, young people are deprived of the opportunity to develop a valuable real-life learning tool.

The built-in learning amplifiers

Evolution has equipped us with some basic habits and capabilities that enable us to amplify and accelerate our learning. One is simply being able to *focus our attention* and zoom in on just that one small part of a scene that seems to be out of line with expectations. (It is that single bored-looking face in the middle of an otherwise receptive audience that keeps me trying to improve my delivery.) If you can tune small areas of the neural network, rather than having always to work on the big picture, learning is more targeted and more efficient.[113]

Another built-in amplifier is the disposition to go looking for learning – to be *curious* and inquisitive. Very simple learning creatures like an amoeba just register what comes their way; but more complicated animals like us can be even better prepared to deal with the future if we have done a bit of targeted reconnaissance. We are not just problem-*solving* creatures; we seek out and if necessary invent problems that stretch our competence and capacity to respond to novel events 'just in case'. Don't just wait for that funny-looking creature to reveal, in its own time, whether it is friend or foe; get a long stick and gently prod it, and see what happens.

A further pair of built-in learning amplifiers are *practice* and *play*. Even when there is no immediate need, toddlers will try again and again to 'get it right', whether 'it' is sounding a tricky consonant or stacking some blocks. Taking time to hone your skills so they become smoother, more reliable and more economical makes good evolutionary sense. Practice makes perfect, and the disposition to practice seems to be built in to the brain.[114]

But if all we did was learn to 'do it right', we would run the risk of our expertise becoming robotic and stereotyped. Practice by itself can make us fluid but inflexible, vulnerable when the world, next time, throws a curve ball and the situation turns out to be different from the one we have been so busy getting ready for. So natural selection has favoured those who have discovered how to balance practice with play. In play, you deliberately mess it up a little, or try something different, just to see what happens. Of course you don't do this when the stakes are high, in the middle of the exam or the Cup Final. Play often takes place 'off-line', in situations where the risks of messing up are reduced, or in scaled-down simulations of the 'real thing' (as in play-fighting between tiger cubs, or children). But the disposition to explore wider possibilities and experiment with different reactions builds in flexibility and creativity alongside well-practised efficiency and economy.[115]

Imitation and inhibition

Probably the two most powerful built-in amplifiers of learning are *imitation* and *inhibition*. The human brain is disposed to imitate – much more so than any other animal, though many other species learn by copying too. (Queen Elizabeth II is reputed to have said, 'I learned the same way animals do: by watching their parents.') Neuroscientists have recently discovered that our brains are wired for imitation: I am automatically primed to do the same thing that I have just seen you do. Children are such natural and compulsive mimics that they copy a modelled behaviour more faithfully than chimpanzees do – even when it is obvious that there is a more economical way to do it. If I model opening a box to get a banana in an unnecessarily complicated and roundabout way, the chimps cut to the chase: all they care about is getting the fruit. But toddlers will reproduce all the movements – not because they are stupid, but because they are more likely to trust that there is method in the adults' apparent madness that they can't yet see.[116]

Imitation is the biological key to the vast treasury of cultural learning, because through imitation, children are able to pick up all the culturally-laden habits of those around them. Through imitation they learn language, and discover the enormous potential for learning that reading and writing, as well as talking and listening, bestows. As children learn, through observation and modelling, how to talk like the grown-ups around them, so they are, largely unwittingly and without conscious effort, absorbing the values, habits, beliefs and understandings of their cultural world. How to tell a story, who to hate, how to hold your knife, what to ignore, how to disagree –every moment, children are being sculpted by the irresistible urge to copy the actions of their elders and thus, very importantly, take on the inferred goals and beliefs behind those actions.[117]

The second of these two pivotal learning amplifiers draws on our brain's extraordinary ability to inhibit itself. The human brain differs from that even of our closest genetic relatives, the primates, in having massively enlarged frontal lobes. For a long time, it was not known what function these might serve, but we are now beginning to understand them. What they seem to do is coordinate and control the rest of the brain, and they do this largely by dampening and delaying some activities in favour of others, rather in the way that traffic lights regulate the flow of vehicles at busy junctions. Through inhibition, the frontal lobes can 'decide' what, at any moment is to count as a distraction, and by dampening it down, allow us to focus our attention selectively on one thing at a time. Inhibition gives us the ability to concentrate. It also sorts out the problem of which, of a whole range of possible things, we are to do next. It prioritises and sequences our actions, so we don't trip over ourselves trying to do too many things at once. Again, some routine actions can be relegated to the background of awareness, while more complicated or urgent things can be given the lion's share of the available mental resources.[118]

Most importantly for learning, inhibition allows us to try out actions and experiences in the brain without moving our bodies around. Inhibition makes *imagination* possible. The frontal lobes can dam the outflow of activity from the centre of the brain before it actually gets to the muscles, and this enables us to imagine scenes and actions without acting them out 'for real'.

Imagination, of course, amplifies learning hugely. Our brains can generate and sift possibilities without running the risk of putting them into practice. The wealth of experience stored by the brain can then be mined for useful and plausible hypotheses to try out in its own private rehearsal room. (And that privacy may be important too. Real physical trial and error allows other people to see what you are up to, and they might steal your good idea. Although we are all supposed to 'play nicely' and share our toys, in evolutionary terms the quandary of when to cooperate and when to compete is ever present. So stealing a cognitive march on your neighbour by keeping your plans and rehearsals secret for a while may well have been rewarded by natural selection.)

on also expands our ability to be creative, in the sense of with fresh ideas when we need them. An analogy may help to explain how it does this. When we are being purposeful, the frontal lobes help us stay focused by sharpening up the 'grooves' that habit has worn in the brain. Inhibition corrals our trains of thought, and helps us have a 'one track mind' when we need it. Our brain goes into a one-thing-at-a-time and one-thing-after-another mode. In familiar circumstances, this mode is highly efficient. But when logical reasoning and familiar trains of thought are not delivering the goods, then our brains can slow the process of thought down (by damming the outflow again, so you get lakes rather than rushing torrents). These pools of activation can allow more ideas to be active at the same time (though perhaps each one is less bright or clear-cut). And they can also relax the boundaries between ideas, allowing them to broaden out and bleed together. Instead of functioning like a crisp, clear pencil sketch, the brain is working more like a watercolour painted on wet paper. This is the state that I referred to a little earlier in this chapter as reverie, or day-dreaming. In this state, some of what you get is a mess, or non-sense (as dreams often are). But you are also more likely to come up with a novel combination of ideas – a new metaphor maybe – that opens new lines of exploration. To be creative, you need to be able to move between thinking carefully and methodically, and allowing your brain to slip into this more dreamy and receptive state. It is the frontal lobes' delicate modulation of inhibition that enables these shifts of focus to occur.[119]

From intuition, imitation, inhibition and imagination emerges another powerful amplifier of learning: the ability to make your own mental models of how a range of interesting other people think and behave, and then use those models to run *simulations* in your head. Wondering 'what Auntie Pat (or Mahatma Gandhi) would have done in this situation?' is a very useful way of generating good ideas about how to tackle a tricky problem (assuming Auntie Pat to be a good role model, and your simulation of her to be accurate and productive) – and thereby boosting your own learning power. The ability to see the world through the eyes of an interesting variety of other people is a great amplifier of learning. The ability to inhabit models of other people is also the basis of empathy. And while empathy is a deep virtue in its own right, it is also a vital lubricant of social learning. Debate proceeds more productively if the participants have not only the ability, but the disposition, to entertain each others' points of view.

It goes without saying that *language* itself vastly expands our learning capacity. It enables the development of powerful forms of communication, and of disciplined modes of thought. Without language our learning would be immeasurably poorer. We could not email our questions, have heart-to-hearts with our friends, mull over drafts of letters or documents, consult the dictionary or use Google to search the internet. But neuroscience is sending educators a strong reminder that language and logic are not the be-all and end-all of learning. Intuition, imagination and empathy are just as important, and they remain so throughout life. It is a mistake to suppose that these non-verbal learning amplifiers are somehow inferior or more primitive, to be outgrown and discarded once language and logic kick in. When you add trumpets to an orchestra, it is foolish to suppose that the strings have to be kicked out, and when disciplined thinking comes on line, you do not have to remove imagination. Far from it: they form a very powerful duo when they learn to work together.[120]

Piggy-backing on our evolutionary gifts, cultural experience enables us to pick up a number of powerful methods for boosting our own learning. Many of these enable us to learn more effectively with and from other people. A person who can choose good role models and likes to watch them at work is expanding their own learning. A person who can talk openly about their concerns and half-baked ideas to the right sounding-board is expanding their learning. Someone who can take well-meant feedback without getting defensive, and who can give other people feedback graciously and appropriately, is expanding their own ability to learn. Someone who listens carefully and connects with other people's ideas and frames of reference makes a better member of a working team, and gets back as much as they contribute. People who know when to lead and when to hold back help to create groups that can explore effectively together. Someone who can create their own best balance between getting input and ideas from others, and quietly sieving and exploring those ideas on their own, is a better learner than the compulsive talker or the painful recluse. The social skills of debate and dialogue are essential to effective learning.

Enhancing (and stunting) the capacity to learn

So far I have only given a very basic outline of the learning amplifiers and transformers. But the critical point is that each of them, singly and in combination, is capable of continuous development. We can expand our learning power over the course of months and years. Or we can contract it. Each of the learning amplifiers can be neglected and stunted. The ability to pay detailed attention to a rock pool, a computer screen or the night sky, for example, can be cultivated, or it can be coarsened. Powers of concentration can be strengthened or weakened, depending on the activities someone regularly engages in, and the examples that are being set by people around them. The ability and the willingness to put yourself in someone else's shoes can be developed, as can the readiness to use imagination, and the patience to ruminate. But we can also grow more egocentric and more impatient. Writing can be developed into a sophisticated learning tool, making increasingly skilful use of notes, diaries, filing systems and drafts; or the very process of writing can be made onerous and hateful. The skills of listening and debating can grow or shrink. The ability to accept feedback without getting upset or defensive can be practised. Listening well is an art that every new counsellor has to learn, and every schoolchild can be taught. So science tells us that 'learning to learn' – focusing, expanding and transforming that wonderful natural learning ability with which we were born, and taking it to new heights – is a real possibility. Learning itself is learnable.

And it is also teachable. Science is helping us begin to understand what the right conditions are for growing powerful young learners. Some direct instruction and discussion is very useful. It helps if the rich, variegated nature of learning is talked about in schools, and by parents, not least because it helps to break up the dysfunctional belief that 'proper' learning is only what happens behind desks. Young people need a broad conception of learning, and they need to see how the learning they do in school connects with all the learning they are doing

elsewhere (but may not have thought of as such). More than that, ‚
need a vocabulary for talking about how learning happens, and what
good learners are like. We'll come back to that in a minute.

However, merely talking about learning is not going to breed better
learners. The point is not to turn out kids who are knowledgeable
about learning, and who can tell you what the 'multiple intelligences'
are. As we have seen, it is a blind alley to put a lot of effort into creating
separate courses on learning or thinking that teach children *about*
learning, if that knowledge does not translate into action. The aim is to
grow the habits of mind that will make them natural good learners
wherever they find themselves. Some knowledge helps, but it does not
magically transmute into competence by itself.

The language of learning needs to become the dominant discourse
of schools. If young people do not know how to talk about the process,
the feelings and the trials of learning, it is hard to interest them in how
they might get better at it. In hundreds of classrooms, as we shall see in
the next chapter, you will hear not 'Get on with your work' but:

- 'How are you going to go about that?'
- 'What is hard about that?'
- 'How are different groups going about that?'
- 'How else could you do that?'
- 'What could you do to help yourself if you get stuck?'
- 'How could you help someone else learn that?'
- 'What are the tricky parts?'

We saw earlier that special training in learning or thinking 'skills' is not
enough. The idea that you can train someone to think in the same way
you can train them to weld a joint or make a white sauce is misconceived. Having the ability is enough, in these practical cases, because
the context usually cues you very strongly when they are to be used.
When you get to this part of the job or the recipe, it is obvious that the
next thing to do is fire up the oxyacetylene torch or melt some butter
in a saucepan. But 'putting yourself in someone else's shoes', or 'trying
it a different way when you are stuck' are not so strongly cued. You
have to be on the lookout for the right occasions; they may not signal

themselves so strongly. The job of schools is not just to get young people to the point where they *can* learn better; it needs to go further, and cultivate the habit, the confidence and the pleasure of learning too. As well as 'able', schools need to work on cultivating 'ready' and 'willing'. That is why expanding learning capacity has to become a deep, abiding intention that permeates the whole culture of a school. Less than that won't achieve the core objective.

But if learning can be amplified, it is also capable of being stunted. There are some false beliefs that young people may internalise that will make them less inquisitive and less resilient , thereby inhibiting their learning capacity. Our first responsibility as parents and educators, therefore, is to make sure that that their learning capacity is not undermined by any false beliefs. The key ones to look out for are:

- *'If I am low-ability, effort will not help.'* As we saw earlier, believing this undermines people's readiness to try hard and take risks. There are various more specific versions of this debilitating belief such as *'I am hopeless at maths'* or *'I couldn't draw to save my life'* or *'Learning is easy (if you are "bright").'* These are not statements of fact; they are self-limiting beliefs.
- *'Learning proceeds on a smooth upward path'* is quite untrue. Learning often proceeds in a jerky and unpredictable sequence of insights, plateaus, regressions and frustrations. If you don't understand this you will struggle more than you need to when the going gets tough.
- *'Learning is Lego-like'* assumes that all learning can be neatly built up in separate, snap-on segments. It can't. Adding pearls of wisdom one by one to an ever-lengthening knowledge necklace is a very rare kind of learning. Much more often, islands of comprehension appear gradually from a general fog, and only slowly begin to join up and make overall sense. Only when students do 'revision' do they sometimes begin to get any 'vision' at all – and often, not even then.
- *Learning can (should?) proceed without mistakes'* is a falsehood that risks making people see mistakes as failures, and exacerbates any risk-aversion they may already have. Trying things out, and not

knowing what will happen, is the essence of learning. Though some mistakes are costly, and experimentation needs to be judicious, the biggest mistake of all is to be so frightened of making mistakes that you dare try nothing new. Some people have even been lead to believe that being confused is a shameful state, so they cling to a thin veneer of certainty, and sacrifice any depth of inquiry as a result. Learning often takes time, and it is smart to inhabit confusion rather than flee from it. As business writer Tom Peters says, often, 'if you aren't confused you're not thinking clearly'. Some forms of confusion are to be avoided, for sure, but to encourage young people to confuse being 'slow' – needing to take your time to master something – with being unintelligent is not very smart at all. '*Slow = stupid*' is a debilitating belief.

Learning to question

One of the most fundamental habits of mind of the powerful learner is curiosity. People become more effective learners as they grow more *ready*, more *willing* and more *able* to ask good questions. Each of these three dimensions of curiosity has to be cultivated.

The first dimension involves encouraging young people to be more *ready* to ask questions; that is, to be alert to the whole range of occasions when asking certain kinds of questions might be a good idea. Sarah asks a lot of questions in English but is virtually mute in maths. Jacek is full of questions in history, but never asks anything in his football training sessions. Sarah and Jacek can be helped to broaden their disposition to be questioning so they are ready to ask, whenever and wherever they need or want to.

Second, learning-to-learn means helping young people become more *willing* to ask questions: that is, to become more independent of external support or encouragement. Ben does ask questions in class, but only when prompted, and only with teachers he likes and feels safe with. Kellie, on the other hand, seems fearless in her desire to get to the bottom of what she is learning, and will persist with her questions even if they are getting a less than total welcome. Good learners – there is no getting away from it – can be awkward and inconvenient, but the fact that the teacher has not got enough time should not result in Kellie's questioning being inhibited. Ben needs to be encouraged to become more like Kellie.

And the third dimension of growth is helping young people's questioning to become richer, more flexible, more sophisticated: in a word, more skilful. They need to have plenty of practice at asking questions, thinking and talking about what makes a good question, discovering why and how a 'good question' in history is not quite the same as a good question in PE or drama. So, as well as lots of talk, young people need activities that stretch and diversify their growing habits of mind.

Activities that make it fun to stretch your learning muscles are the second core strand of a learning culture, after the language. A classroom should be a place that welcomes and discusses students' questions – even if there is no time to explore them all. Yet, most classrooms are characterised by a dearth of student questions and a deluge of teacher questions. Over a whole school year the average rate of student-generated questions is one per student per month. One child, having learned too well by observing his teacher, thought that you had to know the answer before you could ask a question.[121]

Compare this sad, but all-too-common, state of affairs, with the lesson on magnets I described in the preface. There, you recall, the teacher had designed the activity so that the children were being challenged to generate questions, and to think about what makes a good scientific question, and not just to find out about magnets. In that classroom, the children's questions were central, and their disposition to be good questioners was being strengthened, broadened and enriched – all in the course of a 'normal lesson'.

Modelling

Habits of mind are contagious: sometimes, as we have just seen, alarmingly so. So another essential ingredient of a learning culture is modelling. If we want young people to develop the habits of thinking for themselves, using their imagination, being open to new ideas, saying when they don't understand, and exploring real challenges together, then they have to see their teachers doing the same thing. When Albert

Einstein was asked for his views on education, he said he thought the only rational method of teaching was to be an example. And he added: 'If you can't help it, be a warning example.'[122]

Young people, desperate to learn real, hard, interesting things, can find themselves surrounded by adults who seem to *know* a good deal, but never seem to feel the need to *learn* anything new. Traditional teachers modelled pride and certainty in their knowingness, and may also have modelled a kind of dogmatic authoritarianism, masking a nagging discomfort in the face of any hint of their fallibility or ignorance. I remember a physics teacher who became increasingly exasperated at my attempts to understand what 'mass' was. He kept telling me that Newton's Second Law said that Force Equals Mass Times Acceleration, but I wanted to know what mass was 'really'. Eventually I learned that my questions were merely a source of irritation.

We say we want young people to grow up with an appetite and capacity to learn. That means, at the very least, their being able to inhabit the learning zone – where, by definition, competence and control are not guaranteed – with confidence and assurance. They have to be able to say 'I don't know' without shame. In the face of this simple fact, it is puzzling, to put it mildly, to offer them a daily parade of adults who feel that having to 'admit' any ignorance is a threat to their professional identity, and might herald a 'loss of respect'.

Of course young people need to know things; of course teachers know more about some of those things than young people do; and of course the internet is not always a reliable alternative. Of course I want my surgeon to be knowledgeable and competent. But I am safer in the hands of a doctor who is still an enthusiastic and unashamed learner than I am with one who closed her mind to new things thirty years ago. And my children are better off in the hands of a teacher who is continually open to wonder and puzzlement than they are being hectored by someone who lacks the honesty and courage to acknowledge a mistake or a doubt.

Powerful learning is more than just a 'skill'

Learning happens, in school as in life, on many levels at once. On the surface, most visibly, there is what we are learning *about*: the topic or problem-in-hand. At the moment, I am learning about broadband, cooking on an Aga, fixing the strimmer, and the names and functions of ever finer bits of the brain. But as I grapple with a particular issue, I am also, just below the surface, you might say, developing some specific skills, relevant to solving the problem. I'm learning how to uninstall and reinstall the software when the broadband modem blinks in a certain way. I'm learning the unfamiliar habit of slow cooking vegetables in an oven. I'm learning how to clean and dry a little spark plug. As well as learning *about*, I am also, always, learning *to*.

Then, if you go down another layer, less visibly and more slowly, I can see that I am also learning how to learn. I am practising more general-purpose, more generic approaches to learning. When do I need to sit down and read the manual or the recipe book? What's the right kind of question to ask? Is it useful to take a break when I am getting frustrated (with the stupid strimmer)? Who could I call? Could the internet help? Each time I google 'anterior superior temporal sulcus' (one of those bits of the brain) I am refining my more general sense of what the internet is good for and how to make the best and most appropriate use of it.

And if I go down still another layer, I find a kind of learning that is even deeper and more slow-moving, like the depths of a large river. I am learning about, and changing my conception of, myself as a learner. What makes me cross? When am I likely to mess it up by being impatient and impulsive? Who am I reluctant to phone for help and why? When do I persist (crossword puzzles), and when do I give up easily (strimmers, sudoku), and why?

At this level some deep learning about the very sense of self may be going on. Someone might be slowly changing their overall relationship to learning and knowing. They might be gaining the confidence to speak in a seminar, or ask a question at a conference. They might be strengthening their feeling of entitlement to an opinion, or maybe becoming more mute and cowed in the presence of authoritative knowers (like premiership football coaches or professors). They might be learning to deal in a more measured way with the dissonance between someone else's smart sounding theory and their own experience.[123]

I have used adult examples to illustrate the levels. But this multi-layered learning is what is happening for every child, in every classroom, in every school, in every moment of every school day. At the same time as they are practising their capital letters and full-stops, or exploring the causes of the First World War, or analysing a poem, or learning the characteristics of the inert gases, their epistemic mentalities and identities are being formed. What we do in schools has a continual, cumulative influence on the habits of mind, the pleasures and resistances to learning, the feelings of capability or impotence, that are gradually being formed 'below the surface'.

Some experiences leave a residue that opens us up, makes us more courageous and resilient, more questioning and imaginative. And some close us down. A steady drip, drip, drip of experience over time that tells you – not out loud but implicitly, and therefore all the more insidiously – that you have no place in the knowledge-making, knowledge-questioning business, that you are not good at it, and have no right to be there, diminishes your learning appetite and capability. Education must be full of the kinds of experiences that, at those deep, cumulative, character-forming levels, open young people up to learning, and leaves them, at the end of their schooldays, brimming with capability and confidence.

When Einstein talked about those residues of education after the specifics have been lost, it was these vital layers he was thinking of. The evidence is that we forget huge amounts of what we have laboriously mugged up for exams within weeks or months of its having served its purpose. The flotsam and jetsam on the surface of the curriculum, even though we netted and examined it for a while, floats by and is soon out of sight. It is the pleasure in reading – or not – and the confidence in learning – or not – that are the critical residues of education.

An achievable revolution

At A-level I enjoyed chemistry greatly and I did well in it, yet now I can recall almost nothing I 'studied'. I can still drag up a few fragments: pH values; atomic weight, something called Avogadro's number, words like deflagrating spoon and stereo-isomer. But what I *can* remember, what inspired and changed me, is the eccentric, inquisitive, trusting example of Mr Shayer, my teacher, who brewed his own ethanol, and seemed only mildly surprised when the beakers returned to his desk empty. I remember the pleasure of being able to find things out for myself, and of beginning to see patterns and make sense of all the ways that elements and compounds behaved. When I went to university to read chemistry, I was bitterly disappointed that the barrage of facts and formulae thrown at me actually prevented me from reaching a real understanding of the subjects we were supposed to study, and I lost interest in the slog of committing it all to brute memory. It's not that the patterns weren't there; it was that I didn't have the skills, the time or the encouragement to find them for *myself.*

At the end of my second year I dropped chemistry and took up experimental psychology. There, as I had hoped, I rediscovered the pleasure, curiosity, determination and imaginativeness that my chemistry teacher had helped to implant in me. The content of chemistry had drifted by, but those learning appetites and dispositions were there, and just aching to find new, fertile content to which they could attach themselves.

Mr Shayer was an unusual teacher, it is true. There can't be that many science teachers who have volumes of published poetry to their credit, or who periodically send their friends a Horace ode, freshly re-translated from the Latin. Michael Shayer went on to become a professor of science education at King's College London, where I was happy to be his colleague for a while, and to experience his challenging and elliptical intelligence again. But we now know that what he did for me can be replicated more methodically, on a much wider scale, for many more students. There are identifiable ways of doing 'teaching' that develop the ability to pay attention, to wonder, to construct imaginative explanations, and to love learning.

7

Cultivating successful learners

Intelligence plus character – that is the goal of true education.

Martin Luther King Jr

Education has always been about developing those lower layers of the mind. As Martin Luther King says, education is, at root, the development of character traits as well as intellect. And being a powerful learner inextricably combines the two. You need determination just as much as you need the ability to reason logically. Insisting that education is about 'character forming' is only to say that patience in the face of difficulty, and the willingness to see someone else's point of view, are essential aspects of the powerful learner's psychological equipment – more important even than the ability to structure a written argument, or to precis a text.

As we saw in the last chapter, every little detail of the way a lesson is delivered, or a school is organised, is a carrier of values and beliefs. In every school, at every moment, pupils are subject to small nudges and invitations to be this kind of person rather than that; to value this rather than that; to believe this rather than that. Education *is* character-forming, but it needs to focus on a new kind of character – that of the confident lifelong explorer and navigator. Perhaps this is where educational reform can find new ground, as yet uncolonised by either the 'traditionalists' or the 'progressives'.

Traditional views of 'character'

Traditionalists rather like the idea that education is character-forming, but the *particular* qualities of character beloved of the old public and grammar schools are no longer appropriate, and need updating. Cultivating the qualities of 'leadership' and 'moral fibre' used to be the core purpose of education in the old public schools. They saw their job as producing the leaders of the future: the generals, the chairmen of boards, the cabinet ministers, the newspaper editors, the bishops. Through sports and team captaincy, the house system, debating societies, prefect-ship, and so on, pupils were coached in how to take responsibility, organise other people, play by the rules, own up, and make decisions. In lessons, they were taught respect for tradition, and the skills of collecting and collating information, marshalling a clear and cogent case, and expressing their views on paper. They were continually coached not just in how to do these things, but in the value and importance of them. This tradition continued, somewhat diluted, into the grammar schools.

In parallel, in the state schools, pupils were being taught the basics of the three Rs. But they too were having their characters moulded. At its worst, the ethos of many elementary schools invited and rewarded only displays of diligence, attentiveness, politeness, deference to authority, punctuality and accurate recapitulation of what had been taught. These 'follower virtues' of the working man and woman were less talked about than the public school virtues, for obvious reasons. The working classes did not need to know that their education was designed to make them uncomplaining and accurate doers of others' bidding. The fact that some of them worked this out for themselves, and that a great many more of their grandchildren now show their disaffection with such a model, shows an upsurge of resistance to an anachronistic and demeaning system.

Not all today's traditionalists admit to the character-forming agenda. There are those who maintain that teaching is straightforward and unproblematic.[124] Some say it is simply about telling. Schools create an orderly and attentive climate, and then they tell pupils intrinsically worthwhile things. Students practise using what they have been told, and they are tested to see how much of it has been 'learnt'. But this is only straightforward if you resolutely refuse to look below the surface. In reality there is a very powerful character-building model of learning going on. It is not neutral or self-evidently beneficial at all.

Figuring out what answer the teacher wants when a question is asked exercises a very specific set of 'mental muscles'. Learning to sit still and not fidget for an hour is not an easy skill to master, and many young people never do. Being able to store and retrieve verbatim information is a knack that some young people get the hang of better and quicker than others. Ask actors how they have learned to learn their lines, and they will tell you about the tricks and techniques of memorisation that they have developed for themselves and borrowed from other people.[125]

Each way of teaching selects, knowingly or not, one set of skills and attitudes over another. Charles Dickens' infamous Mr Gradgrind is in the business of very deliberately coaching retention rather than criticism; stillness rather than activity; deference rather than challenge; obedience rather than initiative; accuracy rather than creativity. By 'telling' in a certain way, he has chosen to cultivate one set of dispositions and neglect another. Every teacher does. It's unavoidable. So rather than pretending that this isn't happening, we need to look clearly at what type of character traits we would like schools to be helping to cultivate.

The character curriculum

I am not alone in thinking that the revival of 'character education' is the way to go.[126] In recent years, many countries around the world have tried to recast the aims of their curriculum in terms of desirable skills and traits. In England, the new (2008) National Curriculum for Secondary Schools begins by declaring:

> We want the curriculum to enable all young people to become:
> - *successful learners*, who enjoy learning, make progress and achieve
> - *confident individuals*, who are able to live a safe, healthy and fulfilling life
> - *active and responsible citizens*, who make a positive contribution to the well-being of present and future generations.

The Scottish 'Curriculum for Excellence' declares, on the basis of a 'national debate' on education, that 'people want a curriculum that will fully prepare today's children for adult life in the twenty-first century'. Therefore, the statement goes on, 'the goal of education is to equip all pupils with the foundation skills, attitudes and expectations necessary to prosper in a changing society'. Fleshing this out, the documents go on to say that the curriculum:

- should enable all young people to benefit from their education, supporting them in different ways to achieve their potential
- must value the learning and achievements of all young people and promote high aspirations and ambition
- should help young people to understand diverse cultures and beliefs
- must enable young people to build up a strong foundation of knowledge and understanding and promote a commitment to considered judgement and ethical action.

In Northern Ireland, the new curriculum 'aims to empower young people to develop their potential and make informed and responsible choices and decisions throughout their lives'. Between the ages of five and eleven, for example, students should be helped to:

- understand their own and others' feelings and emotions
- understand how others live
- develop tolerance and mutual respect for others
- develop a sense of awe and wonder about the world around them
- contribute to developing a better world for those around them
- become aware of the potential impact of media in influencing our personal views, choices and decisions
- be willing to expand their learning and performance throughout their lives.

One of the earliest of these 'competency-based curricula' was developed by the Royal Society for the Encouragement of Arts, Manufactures and Commerce, the RSA, in London. They grouped their desirable traits into competencies for 'learning', 'citizenship', 'relating to people', 'managing situations' and 'managing information'.

By the time they leave school, according to the RSA, students should, for example:

- have learned, systematically, to think
- understand the social implications of technology
- understand how to get things done
- understand and be able to use varying means of managing stress and conflict
- understand how to develop the capacities to be entrepreneurial and initiative-taking
- understand how to manage risk and uncertainty.

An Australian version says that, when students leave school, they should have things like:

- the capacity for, and skills in, analysis and problem-solving and the ability to communicate ideas and information, to plan and organise activities and to collaborate with others
- the capacity to exercise judgement and responsibility in matters of morality, ethics and social justice, and the capacity to make sense of their world
- the knowledge and skills to contribute to ecologically sustainable development.

There is no doubting that these statements of intent really are trying to give young people the 'competencies' from which they, and their communities, will benefit. The trouble is that long wish-lists of such desirable qualities do not, by themselves, get the job done. The qualities themselves are often so abstract and shorn of detail that it is almost impossible to disagree with them, and yet equally hard to know what in practice they mean, and how on earth a busy teacher might go about trying to 'teach' them.

The grandiosity, and in some cases obscurity, of such aspirations is easy to poke fun at. The ex-Chief Inspector of Schools, Chris Woodhead, in his book *Class Wars*, complains that: 'these aspirations are not "competencies": they are what in this cliché-ridden age pass for counsels of perfection'.[127] Indeed, if you begin to unpick them, some of them do start to fall to bits. For example, what does 'have learned, systematically, to think' actually mean? How can I possibly put a tick beside this, for myself or anyone else? Sometimes I think quite well – I think – and other times rather badly. The research shows that we are all, including high court judges and cabinet ministers, subject to biases and errors in our thinking. I don't know any adults, let alone sixteen-year-olds, who have made more than a start on this one. There's little recognition in these curriculum prescriptions of just how much real complexity and inevitable uncertainty is obscured by their fine words.

Nor is there much recognition of how contentious some of their sentiments are. They come saturated with moral judgements that a good many people might question. Whose idea of 'safe and healthy' are we talking about? Is there no place for the joy of daring and risk-taking – experiences which are central to the lives of most teenagers? Where is the 'commitment to ethical action' in the sleaze and self-interest young people hear about every day in the news? Do I 'understand the social implications of technology'? Does this mean: do I understand all the ways in which programmable machines are undermining the traditional craft skills and the personal dignity of farmers, bakers and tailors? Probably not – though Richard Sennett's book *Respect* has helped me to see some of the issues. Have I grasped all the ways in which technology has undermined the age-old human qualities of fortitude and forbearance? A little better, maybe, for having read Neil Postman's masterly book *Technopoly*.[128] I would love to debate these works with a class of fourteen-year-olds – but I'm not sure if that is what 'understand the social implications of technology' is meant to mean.

And how do I go about 'contributing to ecologically sustainable development'? What do the curriculum writers have in mind? Learning how to make a citizen's arrest on an American president for his refusal to sign the Kyoto Agreement and his support for the US petroleum and logging industries? Learning to decline plastic bags when shopping? Refusing to shop at multinational supermarkets? Getting upset about the clubbing of baby seals? Joining Greenpeace? Trying to get our heads around the two topics of technology and ecology alone could take up the entire curriculum.[129]

The school curriculum has often fought shy of such contentious issues, so delivering on these ambitions is no simple matter. The long-standing Platonic preference for secure, rather than contested, knowledge is not going to be swept away by a few fine words, or the odd classroom debate, about 'ethical choices' and 'sustainable development'. These fine statements of curricular intent are a beginning; but they constitute about 1%, at most, of the work that needs to happen, if education is to become fit for purpose. For the fine words to mean anything, they have to be coupled to answers to specific questions like: how, exactly, do we change the way we teach science, coach sports, mark students' work, write reports and run staff meetings?

The biggest block to these new goals taking real root is the examination system. It has been demonstrated time and again that the tests that are anticipated, by teachers and students alike, exert a powerful influence on how the curriculum is taught and learnt. The tail of assessment always wags the dog of teaching and learning. When GCSE and A-level grades have the power to determine a young person's life-chances, it is reasonable for both teachers and students to adopt a pragmatic attitude, and keep a close eye on 'what's likely to come up' on the test. So until the practical rewards of schooling stop depending on doing well in exams that test the grasp of a body of knowledge, the fine words have little chance of achieving the necessary transformation.[130] Unless schools genuinely start to value a broader range of outcomes, the rhetoric is likely to remain just that. If we truly value the development of young people's 'confidence' or 'citizenship', we will have to find ways of showing that progress has been made. And these records of progress will have to be central and unambiguous. Remember that one of the goals of England's new secondary curriculum is to produce 'successful learners'. But does that mean helping children to become powerful, confident real-life learners; or could it be taken merely to mean that we want them all to get good grades? If there is room for the latter interpretation to persist, nothing has changed.

Overall, though well meant, these kinds of wish-lists run the risk of being too broad, too all-encompassing, too grandiose and too vaguely-specified to be achievable. What is needed is a set of more

e realistic and more practical character traits that schools
y deliver. People are beginning to look for effective
right place – the cultivation of character. But what that
character' is needs clearer specification; and it needs linking more
clearly to the realities of young people's lives that we looked at in chapter 1. And once teachers have a more detailed and coherent description
of what they are trying to achieve, they need a lot of specific examples
and ideas about how to tweak what they do in order to help these qualities and abilities grow. They need to have a good idea of what a more
effective 'epistemic apprenticeship' looks like.

What are good learners like?

I've argued again and again that what young people need is the temperament to cope confidently with difficulty and uncertainty: in other
words, to be powerful real-life learners. But what attitudes and capabilities do such people possess? What do good learners do? What do
they enjoy? How do they react when the going gets tough? Ask these
questions of any audience, as I have countless times over the years, and
they will give a description, based on experience, that maps remarkably well onto the emerging scientific picture of effective learning that
we explored in the previous chapter.

There is one confusion that sometimes needs clearing up before
teachers will give their rich picture of the real-life learner, and that is
the confusion between being a 'good learner' and being a 'successful
student'. Given a moment, people will readily agree that you can be a
successful student without having really developed very much as a
real-life learner; and conversely that young people can be very robust
learners in some areas of their lives without being able (or willing) to
translate that into examination success. Remember those 'bright'
maths students who went to pieces when faced with a question they
didn't immediately understand? Good learners and successful students are not the same thing at all.

What teachers – and young people themselves – say about being a
powerful learner, can be sorted into eight broad qualities or dispositions. I call them *The Magnificent Eight*.

The magnificent eight qualities

1. Powerful learner are *curious*. As we saw in the last chapter, children are born curious. They are drawn to learning. They like to engage with things that are new and puzzling – within limits. They meet the world with an attitude of 'What's that?' and 'That's odd . . .' Learners like to wonder about things; how they come to be; how they work. They are open-minded, looking for new interests and perspectives. They like to get below the surface of things, to go deeper in their understanding. They know how to ask good, pertinent, productive questions, and they *enjoy* the process of wondering and questioning. Curious people can be challenging: they may not take 'Yes' for an answer. They may be healthily sceptical about what they see and are told.

2. Confident learners have *courage*. They are not afraid of uncertainty and complexity. They have the confidence to say 'I don't know' – which is always the precursor to 'Let's find out.' They are up for a challenge, willing to take a risk, to try something they are not yet sure how to do. Given the choice, they would rather learn than merely show off how good they already are. Courageous learners can stick with things that are difficult, even when they get frustrated. They are determined in their learning, and can put in hours of hard graft when needs be. They can bounce back from mistakes: they don't stay floored for long. They have what sports coaches call 'mental toughness'. Mistakes are for learning from, not for getting upset about. They are patient and persistent – but they can also 'give up' on things, not because they are afraid of failing or looking stupid, but because they genuinely reappraise the need to know.

3. Powerful learners are good at *exploration* and *investigation*. They like finding things out. They are good at seeking and gathering information. They are enthusiastic researchers. That can mean reading and thinking and note-taking; but it can also mean attending carefully and mindfully to situations, taking time if needs be, not jumping to conclusions, letting a situation speak to them. They know how to concentrate; they can easily get lost in

their inquiries. They like and are good at sifting and evaluating what they see and hear and read: they develop a trust in their ability to tell 'good evidence'. Explorers are also good at finding, making and capitalising on resources that will help them pursue their projects – tools, places, sources of information, other people. They are opportunistic, alive to new possibilities and resources that crop up along the way.

4. Powerful learning requires *experimentation*. This is the virtue of the practical inventor and the ingenious, inveterate tinkerer. They like to try things out, sometimes to see if they work, sometimes just to see what happens. They like adjusting things, tuning their skills, and looking for small improvements. They enjoy looking at their 'work in progress' – a garden bed, an essay, a guitar riff – and seeing how they can redraft and revise it. They know how to do 'good practice', and how to extract the most learning from their experience. They say 'Let's try . . .' and 'What if?' They like messing about with interesting material – mud, footballs, PhotoShop, friends – to uncover the potential of materials, situations and people. They know how to 'prod' things, to get them to reveal themselves. They are happy to try different approaches, to mess things up, make mistakes, if they are not too costly and if they think they might be informative.

5. Powerful learners have *imagination*. They know how to use the creative test-bed of their own inner worlds to generate and explore possibilities. They know the value of running 'mental simulations' of tricky situations to see how they might behave. They are also good at mental rehearsal, practising and smoothing their own performances in their mind's eye. They know when and how to make use of reverie, how to let ideas 'come to them'. But they have a mixture of respect and scepticism toward their own hunches, intuitions and 'feelings of rightness'. They give some credence to these feelings, but also know they need testing and checking out. They like finding links and making connections inside their own minds, and they use a lot of imagery, analogy and metaphor in their thinking. They know when and how to put themselves in other people's shoes; to look at the world from perspectives that are not their own 'natural' ones.

6. The creativity of imagination needs to be yoked to *reason* and *discipline*, the ability to think carefully, rigorously and methodically; to analyse and evaluate as well as to take the imaginative leap. Powerful learners are good at hard thinking; they are able to construct and follow rigorous trains of thought. They ask 'How come?', and are good at creating explanations that are clear enough to lead to fresh ideas or predictions. They have the ability and the disposition to spot the holes in their own arguments, as well as other people's. Disciplined learners can create plans and forms of structure and organisation that support their learning – they know how and when to be methodical – but they stay open to serendipity, and are perfectly willing to think again or change their plan if needs be. Disciplined thinking enables knowledge and skill to be used to guide learning, to allow the painstaking process of 'crafting' things, balancing the more creative 'brainwaves'.

7. Powerful learners have the virtue of *sociability*. They know how to make good use of the social space of learning. They are happy collaborating, and good at sharing ideas, suggestions and resources. They are good members of groups of explorers; but, more than that, they can help groups of people become really effective learning and problem-solving teams. They have the knack of being able to give their views and hold their own in debate, and at the same time stay open-minded. They can give feedback and suggestions skilfully and receive them graciously. They are keen to pick up useful perspectives and strategies from others. But they are also socially discerning. Effective learners seem to know who to talk to (and who not), and when to talk (and when to keep silent) about their own learning. They are good at judiciously balancing sociability with solitariness: they are not afraid to go off by themselves when they need to think and digest.

8. Powerful learners are *reflective*. They not only think carefully about the object of their learning; they are able to step back and take stock of the process. They can say 'Hold on a minute; how are we going about this? What assumptions have we been making?' They will routinely mull over their own modus operandi and consider alternative strategies and possibilities. They somehow know

when these moments of taking stock are useful, and they don't get stuck in the trap of being over-reflective: too analytical or self-critical. Good learners are self-aware, interested in contemplating their own habits, strengths and weaknesses as they go about learning, and able to think strategically about how they can become even stronger and well-rounded in their approach. They have a rich vocabulary for talking about the process of learning – for example, when and how they learn different kinds of things best – and also about themselves as developing learners. They see themselves as continually growing in their learning power and capacity. They don't get stuck in a view of themselves as 'bright' or 'average'.

One of the virtues of this list is that it balances specificity with generality. If we don't specify clearly what the learning qualities are that we want young people to have, teachers and parents won't know what they have to do to help them develop. Words like 'creativity' and 'curiosity', by themselves, are a bit nebulous. But if we unpack them into practical behaviours like 'asking good questions', or 'using mental rehearsal', it begins to become more obvious what we might do – and what we might stop doing – to coach that development.

On the other hand, we want the specification to be broad enough to cover many of the most common and interesting kinds of out-of-school learning that young people do. As we have seen, school learning is, in many ways, a rather odd kind of learning that may not recur, all that often, in young people's lives after school. So 'mental toughness' is as valuable on the sports field as it is in an examination hall. Being able to look at the world through other people's eyes is useful in history and drama, but it is also valuable as you prepare for a badminton match against a known opponent, or as you create a piece of music. (Composer Errolyn Wallen has to imagine being a member of the audience, listening to her composition being performed, as she is composing it.)[131]

Over the last fifteen years or so, several researchers have proposed lists of desirable learning dispositions such as the one I have just proposed. Reassuringly, they turn out to overlap to a considerable extent. Some core qualities recur repeatedly, like being adventurous and inquisitive, thinking both systematically and imaginatively, being independent and self-evaluating, being open-minded and non-defensive; being able to listen and empathise, being reflective and self-aware. All the qualities on my list are included by at least one of these researchers, so it seems as if we are getting closer to a consensus about what the habits of mind are that go to make up a powerful learner.[132]

The learning gymnasium

We have already critically examined two of the 'buried metaphors' that have been powerfully guiding and constraining our thinking about schools – the monastery and the production line. If we are to shift our view of what schools are for, and start thinking of them principally as places that stretch and strengthen the capacities that underpin confident learning, we need new metaphors that make that way of thinking seem natural. We need concrete images to animate the rather abstract notion of the epistemic apprenticeship.

One possible alternative is the idea of school as a 'learning gymnasium'. The Learning Gym is the place where children go to have their 'learning stamina' developed and their 'learning muscles' stretched – not, principally, so they can do better in the exams, but so they can be confident, capable, powerful learners for the rest of their lives. This metaphor can lead our thinking in new and valuable directions.

Just as people go to a real gym to develop their physical fitness, so students go to school to develop their learning 'fitness'. Just as bodies can become fitter, so, as we have seen, can minds. Just as being physically fit serves as the 'platform' on which a whole host of different skills and accomplishments can be built, so learning power is the generic launch-pad that allows people to go out and learn whatever they want or need to. At the core of the learning fitness approach is the belief that it is a good thing to have a resilient, inquisitive, flexible, open, convivial mind.

So the Learning Gym's three key ideas are:

1. There are a set of positive learning dispositions and capabilities – the 'learning muscles' – which it is useful for all young people to have.

2. These learning muscles can be systematically exercised and cultivated.
3. It is one of the core purposes of education to do that cultivating.

Just as fitness is a compound idea, comprising stamina, strength, flexibility, weight, speed of recovery from exercise, and so on, so learning power is composed of curiosity, courage, exploration, experimentation, imagination, reasoning, sociability and reflection (those eight Magnificent Qualities). This gives us the basis to start thinking about what kinds of activities might be effective at strengthening the disposition to collaborate, or to persist, or to be self-aware as a learner. How do you make school a place where the whole set of learning muscles is exercised, and therefore developed?

Though bodies come in all shapes and sizes, they can all get fitter. And so can minds. There may be some hypothetical limits to how strong, fast or supple we can get – we are not all as fit as a professional athlete – but that doesn't mean we can't get fitter, nor that there is not enormous potential for us to do so. So in the learning power school students' focus is on developing their personal 'learning stamina' – not giving up when they can't immediately do a maths problem, or read a word, say – and not comparing themselves to how the person next to them is doing. They may say '*My* aim is to get better, over time, at doing what *I* can,' and the level at which they start is a very poor predictor of how well they will do. The key 'performance indicators' of developing physical fitness are increases in your 'personal best'. You run four kilometres in less time. You can lift a twenty kilo weight fifteen times, when a month ago you could only do it ten times. Likewise, developing learning power is best assessed by comparing yourself with your own earlier performance, rather than against group norms or fixed criteria. Research by my colleagues at Bristol University has shown that seeing how your own learning power is expanding over time is much more motivating than being told that you have moved up or down the class league table.[133] There is no room for a self-limiting concept of 'ability'. The fact that someone may never win an Olympic gold medal shouldn't stop them training – for pleasure, for personal satisfaction, for their own well being, or simply because they want to.

What 'exercise' is appropriate is entirely dependent on a person's starting fitness level. For one, a long brisk walk is what is needed, for a recovering stroke patient, a few steps may be challenging enough. Similarly, schools have to be organised so that students can moderate the level of challenge that an activity poses, so they are getting a comfortable stretch, but not being pushed too far. A teacher cannot possibly know each student well enough to do this for them all, and encouraging them to do this moderating for themselves also develops their independence and self-awareness. Research shows that students, at all levels, but particularly adolescents, like having some choice, responsibility and control over their learning, and they will make easy activities harder for themselves, if they are allowed to. They want to have things they can 'get their teeth into'. Unless activities 'stretch' the system, regularly pushing it towards its limits, they do not develop general fitness.

Working on the same muscle group day after day, even if the activities vary a little, does not develop general fitness. Likewise, education for mental fitness has to vary the *kinds* of learning that students are doing in order to build all-round learning power. To solve this problem fitness centres have a range of equipment that encourage different kinds of exercise to contribute to the cultivation of all-round fitness. Weights build strength, the treadmill develops stamina, floor exercises build flexibility, and so on. In the Learning Gym, the curriculum is a well-chosen, varied set of mental exercises. 'Knowledge' is what gives your mind a satisfying work-out. Each subject discipline and topic has to justify its inclusion on the grounds that it affords a kind of mental exercise that is complementary to all the others.

Thus, prioritising the development of children's learning power does not mean that 'content' is neglected. It may mean, though, that the content is selected and used on the basis of the kind of exercise it invites and affords, and not (exclusively) on the basis of 'intrinsic worth' or 'teachability'. From this viewpoint 'mathematics', for example, is a set of apparatus, in one part of the mental gymnasium, that affords and invites certain kinds of mental work-out. Maths teachers will have to be able to answer the question: what learning muscles do quadratic equations or geometrical proofs exercise, that other subjects and topics can't? When looked at in this way we might see that some maths topics duplicate the kind of work-out that is provided by 'science', say, and in a less engaging fashion. This would call into question the 'value' of those maths topics and thus their place in the curriculum. There is no room for different-looking bits of knowledge-kit that essentially duplicate each others' roles.

Getting fitter requires sustained commitment. 'Binge exercising' – renewing that gym membership and going five nights a week for the first fortnight of January, only to have totally lapsed again by the beginning of February – is of no long term use. Gentle persistence, and slowly pushing the limits of your stamina and strength, are what works. Likewise, developing 'learning power' takes time. There's no substitute for sustained work in developing mental fitness.

A physical coach helps you monitor progress, and suggests activities and programmes that will help you narrow the gap between current and target performance. So does a learning power coach. Feedback should be useful and precise, not global and vague, helping students to focus on one aspect of their developing learning power at a time, so they are not overwhelmed by how much there is to do. Recent research, for example on 'formative assessment' and 'assessment for learning' by Paul Black, Dylan Wiliam and their colleagues, has identified many practical ways for teachers to do this.[134]

Sometimes, provided the main focus is on improving personal best, a bit of 'healthy competition' can be useful – as it is in a group of athletes in training. If you belong to a 'team', all of whom, at their own levels, are trying to get fitter and more skilful, competition can help to sustain motivation, and boost pride in progress. In a good team members support each other, challenge each other, and celebrate each others' (maybe very different) achievements. You keep at it because you don't want to let the others down, or because you want to be able to do what they can do. The smart learning power coach, like the physical coach, should be aware of and seek to foster this team spirit and camaraderie. The coach could notice and acknowledge both commitment and progress, and encourage the students to do the same with each other. In several of the schools I have worked with, pupils now continually notice each others' progress as learners, and nominate each other for an award as star persister, questioner or collaborator of the week.

Trainee athletes have the ultimate responsibility for whether they exercise or not, although their coach may remind them of their goals. Likewise, the learning power coach can remind students of the value and purpose of stretching their learning power, and make the exercises as attractive as possible. But the coach can't make them learn, and, ultimately, won't try. Paradoxically, many teachers have found that, when they stop dragging their students so forcibly towards the examination line, young people are likely to rediscover their own motivation and sense of responsibility. And the ones who don't would not have done very well anyway.

Effective coaches model their own skill and commitment in raising their own level of fitness. They are not afraid to be red in the face and out of breath, alongside their trainees. Analogously, learning power coaches see the importance of modelling and demonstrating learning-positive habits of mind. They are happy to say 'I don't know' or 'That's a good question; how could we investigate that?' They miss no opportunity to model confident enjoyment in being an enthusiastic learner. Allan Schoenfeld, an American mathematics educator, for example, regularly invites his students to throw tricky maths problems at him, and models not only skill in mathematical thinking, but also enjoyment in the process of trying to figure things out, in public.[135]

The amoral learner

Some people worry that the aim of building powerful learning muscles might be rather amoral. We are not specifying what young people should be learning *about* and there is a concern that without such 'moral' guidance, young people might become brilliant at learning about bomb-making or white-collar fraud, just as a very fit person might use their fitness to become a skilful cat burglar. It is a theoretical risk, I agree, though nobody, to my knowledge, has used that as a reason to ban PE from the curriculum. The fact that a few international terrorists have been through the British school system has not led to calls for schools to be scrapped.

My article of faith is that the vast majority of people who are confident, capable, creative learners – who are able to think for themselves, and are not frightened by difficulty or complexity – won't use that capacity to make bombs. Fundamentalism throws a rope to people who are culturally floundering. If young people know how to swim, they are less likely to grab that lifeline.

The Exploratory

Like all analogies, the Learning Gym has its limitations. The brain isn't really a muscle, and ideas like 'learning stamina' and 'learning power' are only metaphors. To some people the Learning Gym model sounds too methodical, too predetermined or too earnest an approach to teaching and learning. It lacks a sense of adventure, of fun, even of mystery. It does not put the young people and their various interests and talents near enough to the centre of the enterprise. For other people it can sound too individualistic, lacking in the vital social dimension of learning.

To offset such doubts, we could explore a complementary image: the school as Exploratory. The Exploratory was the name that the great cognitive scientist and philosopher Richard Gregory gave to the first hands-on science centre in the UK. As an observatory is a place to go and watch things, so an Exploratory is somewhere you go to explore things. Exploratoria are for everyone, not just professional scientists. The first physical Exploratory was founded in Gregory's home city of Bristol. Its exhibits, or 'plores' as Gregory called them, surprised and intrigued visitors, stimulating them to investigate for themselves the natural and human worlds. They could play with visual illusions to see what made them work. They could see what happened when friction was removed from a micro-world. Exploratories are places for thinking, experimenting and arguing, not just for looking and reading. Could schools be Exploratories, full of 'plores' that stretch, challenge and perplex young people? Could they be places where young people go to develop the minds and temperaments of explorers: where they will learn to be adventurous and pioneering, to relish challenge and assess risk, to enjoy struggling with genuinely hard stuff, and to formulate their own projects and build their own teams? It takes courage, skill, judgement and camaraderie to venture into the unknown and those are the qualities that underpin the capacity to live a happy and fulfilling life. Could schools give young people the adventurous and confident spirits they need?

One of the things the Learning Gym analogy does not bring out strongly is the idea that young people should be learning not just *how* to explore, but *what*. At the same time as they are building their learning capacities and dispositions, an Exploratory should be a place where students are also becoming more and more responsible for creating their own explorations. If school Exploratoria could offer a wide variety of plores – rich and varied sites for exploration, all of which are genuinely valued – they would allow young people to find out what particular kinds of explorations attracted them most strongly.

Some people like physical challenges like sky-diving and potholing. Some like to develop skills like football or playing the guitar. Some like mastering difficult bodies of knowledge. Some like finding out about other people. Some like the kinds of emergencies that confront traffic police or A&E nurses. Some like the slower, more painstaking challenges of writing stories or making animated cartoons. Some like to stick to one kind of exploration, and some like to have a portfolio of different kinds on the go. Some people quickly find a passion for life, and some take longer to 'mill and churn', as the OECD says, trying a range of different things for longer.[136] The range of learning preferences and possibilities is enormous – and a good Exploratory should be rich enough to give any young person a taste of different kinds of exploration. It is, of course, 'administratively inconvenient' – but dozens of large and busy schools are managing to take real steps in this direction.

Perhaps this is where Howard Gardner's multiple intelligences (MI) come into their own. Maybe being logical-mathematical, linguistic, musical, kinaesthetic, interpersonal and the rest are not so much kinds of intelligence, but simply different domains in which one can become a proficient explorer. If the MI framework can help to recover some of the 'parity of esteem' in which these different kinds of domain ought to be held, it will have done a good job (regardless of how robust it turns out to be as a scientific theory of the mind). If the idea that there are many different ways to be intelligent helps young people discover and value their own preferred exploration zones, then it is a useful idea. Exploratories are places that help you find out where your talents and passions lie: what it is you want to become good at.

Back in the 1970s, when I was starting out on my academic career, educators used to get very enthusiastic about something called 'discovery learning'. Discovery learning was supposed to mean that students were given the opportunity to be active explorers, rather than passive recipients. Unfortunately, what they quickly found out was that at the end of the lesson the teacher would tell them what it was they were supposed to have discovered. For forty-five minutes students went through the motions, in science for example, putting different amounts of the green stuff into 25 ml of the clear stuff, and then the teacher would draw the results they were supposed to have got on the board, and the students copied it down. As one student told me at the time, 'The conclusion of your lab report is where you explain what *should* have happened.' Young people quickly discovered that if they out-waited the teacher, they would eventually be told the right answer – the information that the examination would require them to produce. They were still on the Assembly Line, albeit one thinly disguised as an Adventure Trail.

The Exploratory is different. One of its essential features is that the problems are 'real'. The fate of discovery learning taught us that it is vitally important, to students' engagement, that they are genuinely knowledge-making rather than knowledge-consuming. And the skilful teacher offers projects that are rich in exploratory potential, and which enable students with different degrees of learning power to find a comfortable level of 'stretch' for themselves. Finding and presenting such plores – what David Perkins calls 'wild topics' – is skilled work. Like the original Exploratory in Bristol, the exploratory school environment needs to be carefully designed.

In Phoenix Park High School, for example, maths is taught through very open-ended questions and projects. Students are given simple situations like, 'You have thirty-six identical fence panels. What is the maximum sized enclosure you can make?' Or, 'Play the game *Yahtzee!*

(in which you have to accumulate a variety of different patterns by throwing five dice). Work out the probabilities of different patterns, and devise the best strategies.' They work on these kinds of problems in pairs or threes, sometimes pursuing the same problem for several weeks. Teachers will only give them the specific mathematical knowledge they ask for. Mathematics educator Jo Boaler has found that this sort of teaching has four effects, compared with conventional good maths teaching. Students are more engaged; their GCSE examination results are better; they make much more use of their mathematical knowledge in later life; and they develop greater confidence in general problem-solving.[137]

The idea of the Exploratory also emphasises another aspect of learning that is less prominent in the Learning Gymnasium model, and that is collaboration. The learning gym is a rather individualised concept. Go to most gyms and you may not see much team spirit. You see a lot of individuals pushing their own limits. But the real world of learning is often highly social and collaborative, and both the goals and the modus operandi of schools needs to reflect that. In an Exploratory, as in the maths example I have just given, young people are talking, arguing, questioning, researching *together*. They are stretching and strengthening all the different component muscles in the group I earlier called sociability. To continue the physical training analogy, the learning classroom is more like an athletics squad, or a football team, than a gym full of disconnected individuals trying to get fit.

An Exploratory contains not just problems, puzzles and provocations, but resources for pursuing the explorations, to be drawn upon as required. A prescribed curriculum progressively gives way to self-managed research. An Exploratory is organised not to tell students what they need to know, but to help them to develop their ability to decide who and what can help them, and learn how to select and search for information. There are libraries, indexes, databases, spreadsheets, search engines – all kinds of tools available that have to be learnt about, and chosen between. And then the discovered knowledge has to be understood, summarised, evaluated for validity and relevance, and so on. Every so often, the apprentice explorers may be prompted by their 'guide' to flex their reflection muscles: to take a step back, reflect on how they have been going about the task, what methods or sources of information they might have missed, and where else they might be able to apply the information or the skills they are using. And, gradually, these moments of reflection become second nature, so the prompts become less and less necessary.

Traditionalists might be beginning to panic about the loss of *coverage*. Granted students will be studying, understanding, evaluating and applying some 'knowledge', but the worry is that it will be patchy, driven by the needs of the moment, rather than 'a considered overview of the field'. To which I have to reply: true enough. And it is a price well worth paying. If our attention is forward-looking, focused on the development of young people confident and capable enough to undertake whatever explorations life might ask of them, then the broad, superficial 'curriculum by mentioning' has to go.

In an Exploratory, young people will have a feeling of excitement in grappling with real challenges. I cannot stress enough that young people want do things that matter, that haven't been endlessly worked over before. They want to do things they can see the point of. They want to do things together. They want to feel that, in working on these challenges, they are developing the confidence and capability to face whatever life may bring. And they want just enough help to get them going again when they are truly stuck – and not before.

We have explored in some detail the qualities that go to make a confident learning character. They are valuable in the face of a wide variety of real-life challenges and uncertainties as well as in school. Indeed, they have a very different emphasis from the attitudes and habits of mind that are unthinkingly required and rewarded by conventional examination-oriented education. 'Learning' in the real world is much wider, deeper and richer than the stylised and repetitive activities that sometimes still go on in schools. We should be readying youngsters to relish and engage with that richness, not training them to remember and recapitulate things they have heard or read. Learning is a natural gift: one that is capable of being both cultivated and curtailed.

We now have some fresh ideas and some productive new images and possibilities for how schools themselves might grow. But is this just rhetoric, or are there practical things that busy teachers, working with real kids, under all the pressures they currently experience, can do to give all young people the strong and supple minds they so obviously need? Let us see.

8

The learning power school: success stories of the quiet revolution

A lot of the time at school, and this is really an important point I think, they teach you the knowledge, but they never teach you how to learn.

Nineteen-year-old woman, London[138]

The ideas of the Learning Gym and the Exploratory are intended to open up lines of thought and practical possibilities that are very different from those of the old Assembly Line and Monastery models. But is it possible to turn a real school into a Learning Gymnasium or an Exploratory? Can we reform what we do so that it makes a genuine, and not just a cosmetic, difference to students' experience? Can we engage the energy and enthusiasm of busy teachers, in the face of all the challenges and limitations that schools face?

In this chapter, we shall put some flesh on the bones of the arguments and metaphors, and explore some of the many ways in which real schools are already preparing their young people for a learning life – and, at the same time, getting better examination results. On the surface these schools might look much the same as other schools. Many of the familiar building blocks of education remain: classrooms, topics, teachers, even tests. But each of those ingredients of school appears in a different light when illuminated by new metaphors. Teaching still has a very important role, but the teacher is guide and coach, not controller and fount of all knowledge. There is still 'content' to think about and learn, but knowledge is there not to be 'bolted on' as one component of the 'educated mind'; it is there to stretch, and so develop, a range of diverse habits of mind that add up to a powerful learning mentality. And it is there to help young people find their own learning passions and pathways.

Teaching questioning

Andy Carpenter teaches an A-level Chemistry class at Kingsbridge Community College in Devon. He was struggling to get the students to ask any questions at all. They had lapsed into a deep passivity, in which all they wanted was to be given information to pass the exam. And they didn't like putting their hands up and asking if they didn't understand. So Andy had to try to rehabilitate their wasted questioning muscles. He dispensed with 'hands up', and instead got them to think in small groups about what they needed to know, and to place their questions on Post-It notes on a Question Wall. After fifteen minutes, the class gathered to discuss the questions. Within weeks, their questioning had revived. And not only were they now beginning to flex those slack questioning muscles; they were enjoying the process, and taking a much more active role in their learning. 'They come in at eleven full of questions and ideas,' said Andy, sadly, 'and by the time they get to their GCSEs, somehow we've knocked it out of them. What do we do?' The good news, from his experience, is that with a little ingenuity, and the willingness to experiment with the classroom routines and expectations, you can get it back.

Andy had to re-start his students at quite a basic level, but for young people who have not lost their inquiring minds, metaphors and analogies can be powerful tools for asking good questions. 'How is an X like a Y?' is a question-generating question. How is memory like a library/a hard drive/a stomach/an aquarium/a variety show? How is love like a harbour/a fever/a fox-hunt/a red, red rose?

Students could have a lot of fun with these metaphorically-driven explorations:

- How is education like a factory?
- How is education like a hospital?

- How is education like a soup kitchen?
- How is education like a circus?
- How is education like a gym?
- And how is it not like each of these?

Or:

- How is learning like building?
- How is learning like gardening?
- How is learning like eating?
- How is learning like exercising?
- How is learning like exploring?

Students could learn a lot about 'good questions' by exploring the ways in which such tools are used, and how they drive enquiry in certain directions.

The power of projects

At a conference in Australia held at Melbourne's Glen Waverly Secondary College, I watched some presentations by students on their 'extended enquiry' projects. In year nine, these students have the opportunity to spend every Friday of one term working in a small group on a project of their own devising. One of the presentations was by three fourteen-year-old girls, Surabhi, Stephanie and Fiona. They had been investigating detention centres for refugees and asylum seekers. Having seen such centres on the news, the girls were curious about why they were such ugly and forbidding places. They read reports, interviewed some people who had spent months in these places, and created a sophisticated ten-minute Powerpoint presentation to display their findings.

They were not especially high achieving students, but they spoke with great eloquence and passion about their research. And they explained to us that they were going to carry on their study, but that their question had shifted and sharpened. Now what they wanted to know was, as Surabhi put it, 'Why Australians feel the need to behave so unkindly towards desperate strangers.' Their seriousness moved and inspired everyone in that room. And they told us that the project had greatly expanded their self-confidence, as well as their skills of researching, interviewing, collaboration and presentation. But they would not have had such an invaluable opportunity to stretch and strengthen their learning muscles in most schools. It was only because their school had a different vision of education, and a degree of trust in young people, that they had been given that chance.

I heard later that the girls had sent a DVD of their presentation to John Howard, the then Prime Minister of Australia. They didn't get a reply. But they also submitted their research to an international conference on human rights which was held in Melbourne in February 2007. It was accepted, and was very well received by the delegates. The experience was nerve-wracking – and the girls were very proud of having done it. But more importantly, they became more resilient, resourceful and reflective learners as a result. That is real education. It clearly isn't that hard to organise a school so that all young people get such an opportunity.

I have also been able to join students at St Boniface's, a good, traditional boys' secondary school in Plymouth, who had signed up to take part in the ASPIRE project.[139] There were about eighteen students aged between twelve and sixteen. Their job was to work in teams to design a website for 'The school of the future'. They were constructing a range of games, activities and 'provocations' that would guide and encourage other young people to think critically about their schooling, and to be imaginative about how school could prepare them better for life.

There were varying degrees of sophistication in the way different groups were tackling this challenge. Some of the younger students were finding it hard to think beyond wanting comfier chairs and better vending machines. Others has limited empathy, and were assuming that all they had to do was think how *they* wanted school to be, post their ideas on the website, and hope the rest of the world would agree with them. But many were going deeper. They realised that some of their own preferences would not work so well for girls, or for those from different cultures, and they were struggling with great intelligence and commitment to escape the gravitational field of their own interests and backgrounds. Many were designing impressive sites full of questions, quizzes and games to make the site-visitors really think.

Whatever their approach, there was one thing these young people of Plymouth and Melbourne were all agreed on: these activities were the kinds of things they would like more of. They were relishing the opportunity to work together on a hard problem, and to have their ideas taken seriously. The boys of St Boniface's were finding it an interesting challenge to stretch their 'empathy muscles', so as to produce better provocations for different kinds of visitors to the website. They liked being encouraged to think critically about their education, and were responding with great thoughtfulness and maturity. *That's* how they wanted school to be.

Like many schools at the moment, St Boniface's is a transitional mixture of old and new aims and activities. Much of the rest of their time, it was abundantly clear to them (and their parents) that the real game was GCSEs and A-levels. The challenge for this school was to find ways to make the opportunity that these boys were valuing so much, more widely available and more mainstream. The risk is that this experiment becomes a talisman of innovation, to which visitors like myself are proudly led, that has no impact on 'core business' for the majority. The good work that is incubated in such projects has somehow to be fostered and broadcast so that it comes to infuse the spirit of learning throughout the whole school.

Shifting the culture of a school

Ideally, the commitment to building young people's learning power has to run through the life and work of the school, like the lettering through a stick of seaside rock. In chapter 6, we looked at three of the most important of these strands. First, talk about learning, how it happens, and what makes people good at it, has to become the dominant language of the school. Learning – not merely success – has to be what people chat about, notice and applaud. Second, those habits have to become embedded in the daily routines and activities of the school.

And third, they have to be continuously present in the examples that are set by the adults in the school.

When these three things line up around the core educational aim of creating confident learners, you have a genuine culture shift. Put simply, culture means 'the things we value and believe, embodied in the way we do things'. The culture of a school is all the taken-for-granted ways in which it signals – to itself, to the students, to parents, to visitors – what it cares about. The culture is not what we *say* we believe and value. It is what we act *as if* we believed and valued, day in, day out. Or, more accurately, the declarations of value and belief that you find in a school's pronouncements are a part of the culture, but often not a very potent part. What matters much more, in terms of the development of students' character, are the messages of the medium, as Marshall McLuhan famously put it.[140]

What is often most significant about the school's explicit declarations, from the point of view of forming students' attitudes, is how well those overt messages are aligned with the messages of the medium. Where they match, the rhetoric supports the overall implicit purposes of the school, and that congruence strengthens students' commitment. But where the rhetoric fails to match the implicit culture-in-action then the implicit messages win, and the disparity serves only to weaken students' respect for and commitment to the aims of their school. Many schools these days have adopted the rhetoric of 'lifelong learning', but the day-to-day reality for students has not changed to match it.

Psychologists talk about the non-verbal signs, the little things that give away what someone is *really* thinking and feeling. Twiddling a lock of hair, jiggling a foot, the draining away of vocal energy at the end of a sentence so you can hardly hear what someone is saying: such things are the tell-tale signs of other people's moods and purposes. Many of these signals are emitted unintentionally, and picked up and registered unconsciously.[141] This happens with organisations, as well as with individuals. In helping students to cultivate their learning power, it is these signs that matter most. What are the signs that tell you what sort of learning culture you are in? I'll look at some examples from real schools that I've worked with.

School reception area

What are the first messages that greet someone arriving at a school? Does the foyer look like it is trying to be that of a successful business, with signs of achievement and prestige everywhere? Are there lots of cups and photos of visiting dignitaries? Are there one or two students sitting dolefully waiting to be 'seen' by some person in authority, looking like prisoners on remand? Do students slink through the reception area, apparently fearful or furtive in the presence of unknown adults? Are there notices saying 'No students beyond this point'?

Or, is the reception (partly) staffed by students, obviously proud to be playing a small but real part in representing the school? Is there a display of pictures from the school skiing trip, with a wonderful shot of Mrs Burrows, the Deputy Principal, flat out in the snow, poles and skis everywhere, laughing like a drain? Do passing students look you in the eye and say 'Hello' in bright confident voices. Is there a big banner saying 'We are all learning to learn' – or, as in Nayland Primary School in Suffolk, a home-made traffic sign that says 'STOP: Only Learnatics Beyond This Point'?

It is not hard to identify which of these is a learning school, a place where everyone can make mistakes (and laugh and learn from them), and where students are learning responsibility by being given it, as opposed to an Us and Them world of containment and distrust.

Displays of work and learning aids

What about the displays of students' endeavours that you see on the walls of corridors and classrooms, as you walk around? In one school, there is a wall full of students' Best Work – poems, paintings, or photos of the school play. How do you know it is Best Work? Because it is laminated. Lamination is how some schools signal 'Here is an Excellent Product'. Nowhere in this display is there any indication of the rocky road of learning – drafting, rehearsing, arguing, experimenting – that must have lain behind and underpinned these achievements. As far as the display is concerned, the learning process is invisible, not acknowledged or valued, airbrushed out of this public statement of 'What We Value'.

In another school, like Nayland and dozens more, you will see something quite different. Displays of achievement are accompanied by visible evidence of the journey as well as the arrival. In such a school there might be a photo from the dress rehearsal for the school play with a student desperately trying to open a door that had got stuck, and pulling the whole set down in the process. There could be a painting of an early attempt at a sunflower, when – the pupil will proudly explain, if you are interested – he couldn't get the petals quite right yet, and the yellow wasn't really to his satisfaction . . . but this one is much better, though he now wants to try to get it to look less like one of Van Gogh's and more like the ones he saw in Turkey last year. In this school, the walls make a small but significant contribution to the ethos that says: 'We are as interested in the travelling as in the arriving.'

One of the ways you can recognise a learning power culture is by looking at the objects and displays that teachers have chosen to 'decorate' their classrooms – not only the selection of students' work, but their own aids and motifs. These are the artefacts that contribute to a culture of exploration and growth (or otherwise).

In Julian Swindale's year two classroom, you'll see a cardboard construction on the wall that looks like a thermometer, but it isn't; it's a 'riskometer'. It has a velcro strip up the middle, and down the side are small photos of all the children, each with a velcro backing. Sometimes, before they embark on an activity – a painting, an experiment, some writing – Julian invites the children to think how 'risky' they are feeling, and to put their picture at the appropriate place on the riskometer. Right at the bottom means 'Playing this one very safe. I know exactly how it is going to work. Done it this way dozens of times before.' At the top means 'I'm really going for it. I've never done one like this before. I don't know if I can pull it off, but hey!' This little device invites the children to think and talk about their learning courage, and to gain greater control over their 'risk-taking muscles'. They don't have to push themselves all the time, but it encourages them to see that they can choose how risky they are going to be. They are learning that, if you go for something hard and don't quite manage it – if the colours in your painting end up all muddy, rather than the purple you were hoping for – there's credit rather than shame in that.

The riskometer makes a small contribution towards the growing sophistication of a young learner. Risk management and assessment, as any PricewaterhouseCooper's partner will tell you, is very useful in the real world. To give just one example, a piece of anthropological research on the way that top science labs work has found that they tend to construct a varied 'risk portfolio' of projects. Some of their projects will be safe: they know they can deliver the goods. But these are balanced by a few that are much more risky – where they will be sailing in much more uncharted waters. If one or two of these fail, the reputation of the lab can withstand it. On the other hand, they might just end up with a world-beating discovery. Developing a sensitivity to the spread of risk, and the feeling that you can manage and control it, is a good start. One teacher I was talking to recently about the riskometer immediately said: 'I think we need one in the staffroom! I'll suggest it to the head.'[142]

Another classroom display, this time in use with preschool children, is the 'Learning Leader Board'. Working with a slimmed-down set of the learning muscles, teachers and helpers are on the look-out for moments when any of the children, as individuals or a group, are operating at the 'leading edge' of their learning power. Kasha is helping another child with the stapler, which she has never done before. Jonah can't get the glue in the right place to stick his cut-out hat on, but he is really keeping at it, and not getting upset, as he usually does. Timid Robert has started on something without his habitual anxious check with a grown-up that it is all right. At such moments, one of the assistants takes a photograph or jots down the scenario on a Post-It note, and it gets put on the Leader Board. The board is a public collage of the children's 'personal bests' as learners, and, by making those moments concrete, and giving them visibility and status, the children are encouraged to grow into those characteristics more and more. And they are also inspired by each other's progress to push themselves in ways they might not have thought of. Of course, as with the riskometer, it is fine to coast, sometimes, as well.[143]

In the classroom

Try going in to a classroom, sitting down with a group of students working on an activity, and asking them: 'What are you learning by doing this?' Whether it is a maths problem, a translation or an experiment, in one kind of school they will look at you blankly. One bold spirit might even admit (as in a famous research study of science lessons): 'I don't know what you mean.'[144] Those students are Doing What They Are Told. Professor Dylan Wiliam of London University's Institute of Education tells of asking a student in a maths lesson, 'What are you doing?' and getting the reply 'Page 38, Sir.' The teacher acts as if all that is of value is 'getting through the syllabus' and 'preparing for the exam' – and the students may well get good results.

Ask the same question in Preston Park School, and the students will tell you that they are practising looking for patterns in the numbers and seeing how many different strategies they can find; or they are discussing how to design an experiment that will test two different theories about why boats don't sink – and this will help them think through the consequences of their actions in real-life situations. In schools like Preston Park the point is always evident; and the learning point is always more important than 'getting the work done'. And remember: the maths GCSE results are better in Preston Park than they are at Amber Hill, the good chalk-and-talk school down the road.[145]

In a year three classroom at Christchurch Primary School, the children may point you to a whiteboard in the corner of the room on which there are two cartoon characters: a dog called WALT and a cat called TIB. Each has a speech bubble coming out of its mouth. In WALT's bubble it says 'design critical experiments'. In TIB's bubble it says: 'critical tests help make important decisions'. The students explain to you that WALT stands for 'We Are Learning To . . ., and TIB for 'This Is Because . . .' In discussion with their teacher, they have been helped to understand the point behind the experiment they are carrying out, and thus the students see how this little piece of the learning jigsaw-puzzle fits the wider picture of their development. These young people, you will not be surprised to discover, are more engaged, more talkative and more creative in their contributions, than the ones who are going through the motions. They are keen to exercise their learning muscles, because they and their teachers know what those muscles are, how to talk about them, why they are important, and they can therefore see the point.[146] Even the way a classroom is laid out can either encourage or inhibit students in their learning power development. Quite simple things can make a surprising difference. For example, a primary teacher in a workshop I was running suddenly had a small epiphany. She had realised that she wanted her children to learn to be more resourceful – but she had been storing the dictionaries on a shelf too high for them to reach, so they had to ask her to get them. When she moved them down a shelf, lo and behold, the children started looking up words for themselves, as she had wanted them to. If you want to see whether a culture encourages independence, look to see how much the students can access the resources by themselves – and that can mean freedom to go to the library and look things up, to access the internet in the computer suite, or to go to their 'brainwave spot' when they need to be quiet and think (as Vicki Scale-Constantinou's seven-year-olds are allowed to do in their Cardiff primary school).[147]

The layout of the classroom can give you clues about whether you are in a learning power culture. If the teacher is encouraging the students to take greater control of the social side of their learning, getting to know when they work best with someone else and when they prefer to be on their own for a while you might find that some of the chairs are arranged in groups round tables, while some are on their own at the sides of the room. When the teacher suggests to the children, 'Let's use ICT today,' they know they are being invited to choose whether to work Independently; or Collaboratively in a small group of other children; or at the front in a group with the Teacher. Children are gently encouraged to move around, try out learning in a different way, and to think about whether it worked and whether they liked it. As they do so, they are developing a greater sophistication in their use of the social dimension of learning. Again, there is no false tension between developing students' learning muscles and mastering the content. They are quite happily doing both. The test scores are going up rather than down. And it isn't costing a fortune in expensive kit. Such small changes in the classroom layout and the activities on offer cumulatively shift students' sense of 'what we believe and value', and they respond accordingly.

School councils

Building a learning culture is not just a matter of individual teachers in separate classrooms. Every aspect of school life is important. The student council, for example: who gets on it, what it is for, how its recommendations are responded to by staff, what the students are learning by being on it, and whether they understand why. Does it really succeed in encouraging students' feeling of belonging, of having some significant ownership of and input to what goes on in the school? Are the issues they are 'allowed' to discuss tokenistic, or of real import?

Christchurch School's school council devised their own anti-bullying policy and presented it to parents, all by themselves. In Cannon Lane First School, the headteacher, Reena Keeble, gives a group of children the school budget to look at. Her pupils largely write the school development plan. In those schools, both teachers and five-year-olds can tell you what the point of all their learning is. They know that what they learn by tackling these issues will serve them well in later life. How the school council is set up and used tells you a lot about whether the school is taking 'preparation for life and not just for exams' seriously.

Assemblies

It is always revealing to sit at the back of an assembly, and see what gets publicly noticed, and, equally important, what gets ignored – what kinds of student behaviours and achievements are deemed worthy of public comment, and what attracts censure or congratulation. Are the kinds of traits and habits of mind I listed in the last chapter deemed important enough to get a mention? Is there a round of applause for Best Question of the Week, or Most Improved Collaborator? Does Kelly's piece of writing, in which she stretched her 'empathy muscles' by really trying to put herself in the shoes of someone in Darfur, get a comment? Does Dan get congratulated for a brilliant bit of playground mediation? Does the prize go not (only) to the Best Speller, but to the person who has figured out a good way of Learning How to Spell, and shared it with the class? Do students get to nominate each other for Improvement in Learning Awards, or is it down to the teachers? There are a host of ways in which the message 'We Value Developing Learning Power' can be signalled through regular notice and comment.

A school's indicators of success

What a school offers to the world as its 'indicators of success' obviously reveals what it considers 'success' to be, both for its students and for the school itself. It also indicates how open the culture is: whether it is willing or not willing to set standards for itself which it is not yet able to meet. There are certain statistics which every school has to publish, chiefly the Key Stage 2 national test (the SATs), GCSE and A-level examination results. But beyond that, every school should be asking: how are we proud, or at least willing, to be known? What contributions has the school made to learning in the local community? If there is a sixth form, what proportion of students stay on? How many parents turn up to parents' evenings? For a primary school, what is the proportion of students who go on to their first choice secondary school? What percentage of the budget goes on professional learning and development, and who benefits? How many staff members are enrolled in programmes of their own learning? How many visitors come to speak at the school, and what was their brief? All of these, and many more, could be published, alongside the exam results, as indicators of 'What We Value'.[148]

The last indicator, for example, could directly impact on the students' experience of the school's priorities and beliefs. A learning culture might find as many people as it can to come in and tell their learning stories:

- The parent who arrived in England ten years previously unable to speak English, who now runs her own business.
- A member of the support staff who is a passionate scuba diver: how did he get started, and has he had any scary moments?

- A teacher who was disabled in an accident, and has had to learn basic skills again.

If you were lucky enough to get Kelly Holmes to come and talk, would you let her talk about what it is like being successful, and meeting the Queen? Or would you ask her to talk about how she developed her level of mental toughness, what she has learned about how to do good 'practising', and how her various mentors and role models helped her stick at it? Would you want her to be a Celebrity, or a Model Learner?

Teacher talk

You can tell a good deal about a culture by the language. What are the key topics of conversation and vocabulary that teachers use when they are talking about, and to, the students? If you sit in a corner of the staffroom at break-time, do you predominantly hear tales about students' behaviour, their achievements or their woes, or about improvements and efforts made? What do teachers chat about? The Deputy Principal of one fast-improving City Academy said, in an email to me: 'We have changed the ethos from a school that had [bad] behaviour as its prime concern and talking point to a school that focuses on learning.' What he means is: where people used predominantly to notice and talk about students' undesirable exploits, now they are more likely to chat about their learning, and their development as learners. Of course, in reality, there will be a mixture of things to talk about, but the balance has shifted. As a fly on the wall in the staffroom, you might also want to check out how much teachers use 'fixed-ability' language, referring to students as 'bright', 'able', 'gifted', 'average', 'weak' or 'low-ability'. How strong is the tacit assumption that these are valid judgements? How often does their use get challenged? When more ability language is used, there is less likelihood of a strong focus on the improvability of learning.

'Learning', 'work' or 'play'?

One tell-tale use of language is simply whether teachers use the words 'learn' and 'learning' much when they are talking to students. If they

do, how are they used? 'You'll have to learn these formulae for home-
work', uses the word learn as a synonym for 'commit to memory'.
Contrast that with usages like 'how did you learn that?', 'who had difficulty learning that?', or 'how could we have made learning that easier?' All of these use 'learning' to draw attention to the *process* of
coming-to-know, to its variability, and to possibilities for improvement. You might find that, except when they are writing brochures,
teachers don't actually use the word learning very much at all.

But if they don't talk about 'learning' with their students, what do
they talk about? A small study by Caroline Lodge at the London
Institute of Education gave a rather dismal answer – they talk about
'work'. She found that, out of every hundred times teachers used one
or other of the words 'learning' and 'work' to their students, only two
were 'learning' and the other ninety-eight were 'work'. Here is a good
example of the slippage between the rhetoric of the prospectus and the
reality as experienced by students. It is a rare school or Local Authority
these days that does not pepper its publications with references to
learning – learning to learn, the learning society, lifelong learning,
improving the quality of students' learning, and so on. However, by
the time we get down to regular lessons, it seems that what many students are still hearing is: 'Pay attention to your *work*. Get back to your
work. Get down to your *work*. That's good *work*. How's your *work*
coming on?'[149]

The language of 'work' continually reinforces the idea of learning
as drudgery, and of the value of the product over the satisfaction of the
process. This is hardly language that is going to fill students with a love
of learning for its own sake. The antithesis of 'work' is, of course, play
or leisure: things that are associated with pleasure and enjoyment. In
an ironic twist, an experiment by Ellen Langer at Harvard found that
describing an activity as 'play' led students to work harder at it. When
exactly the same task was described as 'work', they put in less effort,
gave up sooner, and enjoyed it less.[150]

What's in a word? Quite a lot, apparently. At the end of a lecture
recently I was approached by a headteacher who had heard me talking
about this research some nine months previously. 'I went back to
school and talked to the staff, and they agreed to start talking more

about learning to the children,' she said. 'We even banned the word work, just to see what would happen.' She went on to describe what she called 'a little miracle'. 'It worked!' she said, in near disbelief. 'The children are much more engaged and active. They talk more and make many more suggestions.' She told me she was sixty-two and coming to the end of her teaching career. 'This is so exciting, I wish I was just starting out – and I never thought I'd hear myself say that,' she said.

'Could Be' or 'Is'?

There is another tell-tale use of language which I mentioned earlier: it is the balance between 'Is' language and 'Could Be' language. In another of her revealing studies, Ellen Langer taught the same information to two matched groups, using Is language to one and Could Be to the other. 'This *is* what the process is called. There *are* three factors to bear in mind,' as opposed to 'This is what some people have called it. There could be three factors . . .' and so on. That was the only difference between the groups. In a test of verbatim learning, the two groups did not differ. But when they were asked to do something more creative with the information – to use it to explore an unanticipated question – the Could Be group performed far better.

It is not hard to figure out why. If you talk to me in Could Be language, I am immediately in a world of openness and possibility. Could be three; why not four? Some people called it X; what would happen if we called it Y? In this linguistic climate, students' dispositions to be open-minded, imaginative, questioning and reflective are automatically recruited. Could Be is an invitation to explore. But as soon as you tell me that something Is, all I can do, unless I am feeling very awkward, is do my best to understand and remember it. That's all that is on offer in the way of learning.[151]

The traditional school curriculum is full of 'Could Be's that are being misrepresented as 'Is's. We all know that the meaning of a text is a Could Be, and the poet's intention when she used that metaphor is a Could Be. The periodic table is also a Could Be – although I have found that it makes some science teachers anxious when you remind them of this. Science especially is the living world of Could Be, and it can be destroyed by being misguidedly converted into Is-ness. Even '4 × 3' livens up when you treat it as a Could Be. 4 × 3 *is* 12 ends the discussion. But 4 × 3 Could Be a dozen, or a baker's dozen one loaf short, or a cricket team plus the twelfth man, or 6 × 2, or the months in a year, or half a day in hours, or enough fish fingers for Mum and Dad and me, or . . . .

Of course the world is also full of 'Is's. And you do have to know that three fours are twelve. But if we want students to become committed, creative, critical lifelong learners, we need to start talking to them *as if* we mean it; and feeding them content and tasks that invite them to use the learning muscles we *say* we value. Incidentally, Could Be language, used appropriately, does not unsettle even quite young children; they know that the world is provisional and contingent as well as we do. And they are also well able to distinguish between open-mindedness and incompetence. A teacher who says Could Be is not at all the same as a teacher who does not know her stuff.

Reports

The reports teachers write about students for parents are very revealing of a school's ethos. In a traditional school, these reports will revolve around the repetitive use of four tired old concepts: achievement, ability, conduct and effort. My reports were full of comments like 'quiet and well-behaved', or 'must learn to apply himself'. 'He has shown something more like his real form this term' implies 'ability', finally matched by effort. My favourite was: 'Guy can do physics standing on his head, and often does,' which, though witty, reduces merely to a combination of conduct and ability. 'I am sorry to learn he has been rather disobedient with matron' speaks for itself (though I rather wish now I could remember what exactly my misconduct was). Being continually invited to look at your child through these grim filters is not very inspiring, though most parents seem to feel that this shrunken image of their offspring is somehow inevitable.

But a Learning Gym sees all young people, primarily, as *growing learners*, and their reports therefore highlight the development of aspects of the explorer's character. For example:

Khaled is now much more willing to stick at difficult tasks than he was last term. He is more ready to take a risk in the way he goes about learning, though still less than he could. He has found new confidence in his ability to work in different kinds of teams, especially those that do not contain his close friends. He uses his imagination well now, though he could still improve when it comes to systematic thinking. He has become one of the class stars at observation: Khaled always notices little details in his explorations that often spark off interesting discussion. I think his challenge for next term might be to stretch his disposition to be methodical, both in his thinking and in the way he plans his explorations. He is really on his way to becoming a powerful learner – Well done!

Would it not be a more cheerful and encouraging experience for Khaled and his parents to receive such a report, rather than 'His maths SATs were disappointing. He must learn to sit still'?

Teachers as paragons of learning?

I have illustrated a number of the practical ways in which a school culture reveals and communicates itself. It does so through its declarations, and the extent to which these do or don't tally with the other signals of value and belief; through the way it presents itself to the outside world; through the kinds of activities that go on there, and the way their purpose is framed; through what is displayed, noticed, ignored, censured and celebrated; through the dominant discourses and key vocabulary; and through the indicators of success which it has chosen for itself.

But I have kept what is probably the most important till last. The most powerful conveyors of cultural messages – as the research mentioned in chapter 6 suggested – are the adult role models that students see around them every day. In a traditional school, teachers modelled knowledgeability. They were, above all, Knowers. They knew how to do things, and they had the answers. But, for all the reasons I've explained, students now need to become good learners, not secure knowers, and so their teachers need to model learning. Now, it is teachers' professional duty to be visibly, confidently uncertain a dozen times a day. They should be cheerful about the fact that what they don't know dwarfs what they do; that they often don't know what to do – but that they do know something about what to do when they don't know what to do. They do not, of course, deny knowing what they know, and that is probably considerably more than their students (though this is not always the case). But that still leaves them plenty of scope for modelling learning.

If a lesson is not going according to plan, teachers should model the ability to 'think aloud'. I was told by a young teacher at a conference of the time when she did just that – in the middle of a lesson that was being observed by an Ofsted inspector. The students were unexpectedly struggling with her very carefully prepared lesson, so she stopped the lesson, and ruminated out loud about what might be going wrong. She acknowledged to the students that she was a bit nervous 'because of the man at the back with the clip-board', and gradually thought her way through to a re-organisation of the last twenty minutes. The inspector told her at the end that he would grade it a 'good' lesson – 'because I thought that was a very useful bit of modelling you did for the children'. Maybe it was her lucky day; or maybe Ofsted are becoming more sensitive to and enthusiastic about learning power than teachers sometimes imagine them to be.

It should be a requirement, I think, that teachers are visibly engaged in some project that stretches their own subject knowledge (and therefore their own learning muscles). An English graduate might regularly pin up the drafts of a poem he is struggling to get right. A science graduate might be running, in the corner of her lab, an experiment in which she is genuinely interested and for which she does not know the outcome. A design teacher might be seen to be in the process of making something that solves a novel problem. A PE teacher might take class time to practice moves that she hasn't mastered yet. A modern foreign languages teacher might be seen to be learning a new language. An RE teacher might share with her class her attempts to practice prayer or meditation.

Peter Mountstephen is the headteacher of a primary school in Bath. On the first day of every new school year there is a whole-school assembly, and in it Pete tries to play a musical instrument that he has never played before. Last year it was the bagpipes. Currently it's the violin. He makes a horrible noise, and everyone titters. Then he publicly commits himself to learning the instrument during the year. He talks about what learning muscles he is likely to need – perseverance, commitment to finding the time to practice, courage to ask for help, and so on.

During the first week of the term, he makes a point of going round to every class, to ask the pupils what they are going to find hard this term, and they talk about their shared challenges and difficulties. He and the children, and their class teacher, talk to each other as learners, about learning. Then, every month, he brings the instrument back into the school to show everyone how he is getting on, and what problems he is encountering. Pete's commitment is to be very obviously bad at something, and to be seen to be putting in the learning required to get better at it. You can imagine how that encourages the children, and frees them up to be 'bad' at something, without feeling bad about themselves.

All teachers should be seen by their students to be trying out ways of becoming a better teacher. That is, they should be modelling someone who is continually looking to get better at what they do. They should regularly say 'let me try this on you' and 'tell me how it goes'. In fact it is very good practice to recruit the students' help in the quest to improve. It could become quite normal to solicit feedback from students at the end of a lesson about how their learning has gone, and whether they could think of any ways in which the teacher might have made it easier or (more likely) more challenging, or more enjoyable.

At many schools now, students are recruited to help teachers improve their teaching. Reena Keeble, the First School headteacher I mentioned a few pages ago, teaches four-year-olds, and at the end of a lesson always solicits their feedback and advice about how her teaching could improve. Reena is a learner, but, more importantly, she is an exemplary model of learning for those children.

At Villiers High School in the London Borough of Ealing, a group of thirteen and fourteen year olds have been trained as 'student lesson observers'. They work in pairs, and can offer their services to any teacher in the school (who is free to decline). To date, about 60% of the teaching staff have had a lesson observed by the students, and taken part in a structured feedback session a day later. Some staff were apprehensive, but all have found it to be a pleasant and productive experience – not least because the students have learned to be impressively tactful and supportive in their feedback. Headteacher Juliet Strang finds that, when students are offered adult responsibilities like this, the vast majority rise to the challenge with great maturity. Her teachers find they have less to fear, from listening to their young coaches, than they might have imagined.[152]

Students can be invited to help coach their teachers in shifting their language habits. I have argued there are three small shifts that can contribute significantly to the creation of a more effective learning power culture. One is talking about 'learning' rather than 'work'. The second is using Could Be language rather than Is language. And the third is replacing talk of 'ability' with reference to effort, strategy and developing learning power. Not 'Jack, you have a good deal of ability at maths' but 'Jack, what do you do that enables you to pick up things in maths so fast, and are there ways you go about learning maths that you could share with the rest of the class?' Not 'Maisie has limited ability' but 'Come on Maisie, I bet you can do it if you try; let's get those resilience muscles working.' There are classes where this is already the default language, and to those teachers it is second nature. But for many others, old habits are dying hard, and need updating.

The easiest way for teachers to shift these linguistic habits is to ask the students to help. Get them to point out when their teacher inadvertently uses the 'old' words, and, if they like, cheer when she uses a 'new' one. If further encouragement is needed, I have found the use of a 'swear-box' very helpful. Every time you are caught saying 'work', you put 5p in the box. At the end of the first week, there is a share-out and everyone gets a present. At the end of the second week, the 'present' will have become quite small. At the end of the third week, you will have more or less perfected the shift in your way of talking. If you like, you can appoint one student to be your 'Work monitor', another to be your 'Is language monitor' and a third to be the 'Fixed-ability monitor'. Our experience is that students enjoy the job of helping to 'train' their teachers, and take it very responsibly.

Making a virtue of fallibility

Brave teachers could take up an idea that was suggested by the late Neil Postman, an American critic of conventional education. We know, he said, that knowledge is essentially uncertain – an always tentative, always improvable product of fallible human intelligence. And we know that much of education acts as if knowledge were more certain than it is. Teachers, textbooks and syllabuses use too much unjustified Is language and not enough Could Be. So his idea was to appoint the class as a whole to be detectors and investigators of overblown claims to certainty. They are to become Knowledge Investigators.

Postman suggests that, at the start of every new class, teachers should address their students thus: [I have amended his phrasing slightly]

> During this year, I will be doing a great deal of talking. I will be explaining things, answering questions and conducting discussions. Since I am an imperfect 'knower' and, even more certainly, a fallible human being, I will inevitably be making factual errors, drawing some unjustifiable conclusions, and perhaps passing off some of my opinions as facts. I should be very unhappy if you were to remain unaware of these mistakes. To minimise that possibility, I am going to make you all honorary members of an organisation called 'Veracity and Accuracy in Education' (VAccInE). Your task is to make sure that none of my errors goes by unnoticed.

> At the beginning of each lesson I will, in fact, be asking you to reveal whatever errors you think slipped by in the previous lesson. You must, of course, say *why* these are errors, indicate the source of your authority and, if possible, suggest a truer, more useful or less biased way of formulating what I said. Your assessment this year will be based partly on the rigour with which you pursue my mistakes, and the clarity and courtesy with which you point them out. (I have feelings too, you know.) And, to further ensure you do not fall into the passivity so common among students, I will, from time to time, deliberately include some patently untrue statements and attempt to pass off some contentious opinions.

There is no need for you to do this alone. You should consult with
your classmates, perhaps even form a study group that can review
the things I have said. Nothing would please me more than for
some of you to ask for class time in which to present a revised or
improved version of one of my lessons.

A variation of this is to make students honorary members of the
Textbook Patrol. Textbooks are one of the most virulent means
whereby unjustified Is-language is spread. They present an imper-
sonal, cut-and-dried view of knowledge that is quite at odds with the
one that operates in the real world. As we have seen, in most real-life
situations, 'knowledge' is a flexible and modifiable resource to be
drawn on, usually by a group of people, in the course of getting interesting things done. It is what 'we' generate, as we go along, that we
think might be of interest and/or use to us or to other people, in the
future. Knowledge stops having any value if people stop finding it
interesting or useful. History is full of examples of 'dead knowledge'
that didn't get disproved; it just stopped being interesting.

The trouble with textbooks, it would be only slightly unfair to say,
is they are mausoleums for knowledge that has largely stopped being
interesting or useful to anyone but school-teachers. However, as a
preparation for real-world knowledge use, textbooks can be an invaluable resource for helping students learn how to evaluate knowledge
claims and develop their critical confidence. Textbook Patrol is
encouraged to ask:

- How do we know this is true?
- Whose claim is it?
- For what purpose was this knowledge generated?
- What is the unacknowledged vantage point of the textbook
  authors?
- Why are they keeping themselves so carefully hidden?

If such books are not used as objects to be questioned and explored,
then they are anti-educational; as Postman says, 'instruments for pro-
moting dogmatism and trivial learning'. Today's textbooks may be
jazzed up with fancy graphics and cartoons. Maths exercises may be

couched in terms of football scores and internet download rates. But underneath, the old view of knowledge often lies undisturbed and unquestioned.

You could, I suppose, produce computerised 'textbooks', or even old-fashioned printed ones, that contain the seeds of their own deconstruction (reminiscent of the cow in Douglas Adams' *Restaurant at the End of the Universe*, who politely invites you to select and slice your favourite cut of steak from its backside). This self-destructing textbook would contain regular exercises that invited the reader to question the unstated assumptions contained in the previous few pages, and so on. But the fact that it is unlikely to happen means that the job of the human teacher, in encouraging students to use educational material critically rather than mindlessly, will remain, even in the computer age, secure.

The other problem with textbooks, of course, is that, beyond their compulsive use of Is language, so many of them are very badly written, and thus encourage students in the belief that the subjects they are discussing are inherently boring. To combat this, schools could institute a student prize for the most boring bit of textbook-ese – like 'Pseud's Corner' – accompanied by the most alluring rewrite. There are dozens of ways in which students can be encouraged to balance respect for knowledge with critical inquiry, and disciplined study with playfulness; these are not either/ors, the twenty-first century character needs both.

For older students, Postman suggests the following as an end-of-year assignment. I think it would do very well as a compulsory A2-level project.

> Describe five of the most significant errors scholars have made in this subject. Indicate why they are errors, who made them, and who is mainly responsible for correcting them. You will receive extra credit if you can describe an error that was made by the error corrector. You will receive extra extra credit if you can suggest a possible error in our current thinking about this subject. And you will receive extra extra extra credit if you can indicate a possible error in some strongly held belief that currently resides in your own mind.

There are many schools in which this kind of critical attitude on the part of students would be treated as heresy. But there are others where this quizzical, exploratory spirit has permeated even into the science and maths departments; where students are encouraged to sharpen their critical and creative faculties, in just these kinds of ways, on a daily basis. What is pioneering today needs to become the norm for tomorrow.

Does it work?

What is the evidence that these small adjustments to vocabulary, displays, activities, reports and modelling actually make a difference? Do young people reap the kinds of benefit that I am claiming? And what happens to the examination results? The good news is that, as far as we can tell, the exam results go up. Of course, it is hard to establish strict cause and effect. Schools are complicated places: cohorts of students differ, influential staff come and go, policies and pressures change – and all at the same time. But the bulk of the research shows that students who have been helped to be more articulate about the process of learning, and about themselves as developing learners, and who have been shown how to be more independent, and given some manageable levels of choice and control, score better in the tests.

In 2001, the International School Improvement Network commissioned a review of research in this area, the main outcome of which was captured in its title: 'Learning about learning enhances performance.' The report found, for example, that children who were encouraged to be more interested in stretching themselves, and less in merely getting good marks, achieved better, worked harder and liked school more. Their general literacy improved as well as their subject knowledge. And 'these children developed flexible learning and inquiry strategies of wide applicability' – interestingly, much more so than other students who were deliberately trained in learning and thinking skills. Learners encouraged to ask their own questions performed better on later tests. Another study found that ten and eleven-year-olds encouraged to think and talk about their own learning 'were more successful in more complex problems, succeeded more quickly, and employed more effective strategies'.[153]

Overall, the report concludes that, 'For nearly twenty years it has been known that students with more elaborated conceptions of learning perform better in public examinations at age sixteen.' That is, young people who can talk about how they learn – who know about curiosity, courage, exploration, experimentation, imagination, reasoning, sociability and reflection – get better GCSE results. Higher achievement is associated with students' saying things like 'I figured out what it was I didn't know,' 'I don't think I quite get it yet,' 'I'm a bit confused,' or 'Hold on, what have I met before that's like this?' And students who have an expandable view of their 'ability' – who think it is possible to get smarter – out-perform those who think their ability level is fixed, regardless of whether they think their fixed ability is high or low.

These results come from large, well-controlled studies. But small-scale investigations can be just as illuminating. Here are a few results from English schools I have worked with over the last dozen years. In 1997, the first school that took my ideas on, and devised all kinds of ways to help children learn how to learn, was Christchurch Primary School in Bradford-on-Avon in Wiltshire (where the bagpipe-playing Pete Mountstephen was then headteacher). Over the next four years, the percentages of children achieving level 4 and above in their Key Stage 2 SATs rose from 59% to 86% in English, 55% to 86% in maths and 67% to 94% in science. Averaging over all three core subjects, the percentage of children over-achieving for their age – that is getting level 5 – rose from 13% to 40%.

The idea that children who have greater learning power (regardless of their IQ) achieve beyond their years, was borne out by an experiment that Jane Leo carried out with her year six children in St Mary's Primary School, Thornbury, near Bristol. She had been working all year on building their learning power, and after they had taken their Key Stage 2 tests, she gave them the Key Stage 3 maths paper – designed for fourteen-year-olds – to have a go at, 'for a bit of fun'. As you would expect, the papers contained questions on topics which they had not met before, but Jane explained to them that 'by applying your thinking and using what you already know, you ought to be able to have a go at much of it'. The children who were not very good at maths at all were allowed to work in pairs. She allowed the children to ask 'clarifying questions' only, which she answered by encouraging them to trust their own judgement. Jane told me that most of their questions stemmed from not believing that the questions were as easy as they were!

The result? All of the children bar five achieved level 6, which is the expected level for fourteen-year-olds, many of them jumping a whole level over their performance in the actual KS2 tests they taken a week before. The other five, who all achieved a level 5, still improved on their actual SATs performance by at least two sub-levels. Compare this with the finding that 75% of children in regular classrooms who achieve level 4 in Year 6 are unable to reach that level again when they are retested in year seven.

Jane Leo wrote to me:

> I believe that their willingness to have a go stemmed from a year's worth of teaching them how to learn and knowing them- selves as learners. Through Building Learning Power, they know how to tackle a challenge; what questions to ask themselves; how to apply what they know to new situations; how to be flexible in their thinking, not always taking the expected route and being comfortable with that; knowing when to move on to something new and let their brains reflect on a problem while working on something else. They know themselves as learners, and they see learning as a journey, not an end – if they couldn't do a question it wasn't because they would never be able to but that they hadn't seen the way there yet.

Jane commented further: 'For me this side of learning is the key to edu- cation. Content-driven education seems to me to confine learning in boxes, while learning-driven education opens up endless possibilities.' But what did her children think of being asked to do something for which they had not been prepared? We know that many children under those circumstances go to pieces. They feel stupid, panic and get upset. But not Jane's kids. One said: 'Strangely, I really enjoyed that.' (I like the 'strangely'!) Another said 'That was good – it makes you see the links between everything.' A third said: 'I can't believe I could do so much of it – and it wasn't boring!' Another reflected: 'I don't think I always did it the easiest way but I still got there.' Several were a bit worried. 'So what are we going to learn next year?' they wondered.

Helping children with learning difficulties

There is no doubt that young people who are doing OK in school benefit significantly from having their learning muscles stretched, and they respond enthusiastically to it. But what about those who are struggling? Let me tell you about Lemar and Tanya.

Lemar is twelve and concentration is a problem for him. Set him to do a bit of writing and you are lucky if, in three-quarters of an hour, he has managed a line and a half. Neither exhorting nor punishing him did the slightest good. One day, Lemar's English teacher had an idea. She drew a line across the top of his page, and said to him, 'Let's call one end of this line "focused, on task, undistracted", and the other end "distracted, scatty, off task". Now, the game is this: every two minutes, I want you just to put a mark on the line to show where you are, on that spectrum, at that moment.' Lemar agreed to give it a go.

By the end of that lesson, Lemar had written nine lines – a big achievement for him. Four days later the class were doing another piece of writing. As the teacher was wandering round, she saw that – without any prompting from her – Lemar had drawn his own line. What she had done was to give Lemar a tool that gave him some control over his distractibility. He enjoyed the challenge – it isn't so easy to remember to do something every two minutes. The game helped to draw him back regularly to the job in hand. The line on the paper, right under his nose, gave him an immediate visual anchor. The game encouraged him to become more self-aware without being judged: his task was not to try to control his scattiness directly, but simply to observe it. And he was in charge. It was as if he had gained access to some controls in his own mind that had been previously hidden from him. And he liked that. In one small way, that line was a piece of equipment in the Learning Gym, which enabled him to exercise and strengthen his ability to manage his own attention – and thus be a more powerful learner.

Tanya is two years old. She attends an Assessment Nursery attached to a special school in Oxfordshire. Tanya is diagnosed as profoundly deaf, and with autistic tendencies. She is also 'tactile defensive', which means she is too frightened to touch anything. When she started at the nursery she was very passive. She just sat where she was put. She would not hold a bottle to drink, nor touch a spoon, and found it almost intolerable to be touched. Not being able to feel and manipulate things is obviously a huge barrier to a toddler's learning. Tanya couldn't play with things, couldn't try to feed herself, couldn't hold on to someone's hand to try to walk. Because her hand coordination was so undeveloped, she couldn't learn the rudiments of sign language. For many reasons, her tactile defensiveness meant she could not begin to be a resilient or resourceful learner.

Over a period of four months, Tanya was gently encouraged to use her hands. Her carers and teachers spent time stroking and patting her hands, getting her used to being touched. Gradually she was encouraged to feel different textures – to put her hands into a plate of baked beans or a jelly. She was given time to watch both adults and other children who were obviously enjoying these feeling games, and to imitate what they were doing. And gradually the doors of her learning began to ease open. As one of her teachers put it:

> Slowly, as Tanya became less afraid of tactile experiences, she began to explore for herself. This was a huge step forward, and a real achievement. She was now able to explore her environment independently for the first time as a result of her developing resilience. Her entire world opened up. She could choose what to explore without needing an adult to initiate the activity. She began to walk, as she could now hold hands or cling on to a walker. She began to sign, as she knew she had hands she could use. And she began to play, at first on her own, then alongside other children, and then beginning to initiate games with them. Tanya also began to finger feed herself as she was no longer afraid to touch the food. Over the four months, her developmental level shot up from 4–5 months to 28–29 months.[154]

Through the skill of her teachers, Tanya has been given the key to the Exploratory. But without that focus on Tanya as a learner, capable of getting better at learning, her difficulties might have been seen as irremediable. Yes, her level of achievement was originally very low, but her teachers refused to infer from that that Tanya 'lacked the ability' to learn and explore. By helping her to find the key to learning, they opened up a learning life, the potential of which we cannot know.

A cautionary note

The key to educational reform does not lie in grand structural changes, nor even in the introduction of special courses to 'teach thinking'. It lies in the cumulative adjustment of these small, specific cultural signs and of teachers' daily habits. It is the culture that counts, as it is experienced, day in, day out, by the students. Grand schemes have failed, time and again, because they do not have the impact that is needed, at the point where it is needed: in the routine life of classrooms and playgrounds. Gradually shifting these habits is within the power of every teacher and every school. But, like any habit change, it requires perseverance. It is no good having a quick flurry of activity one term, and moving on to something else the next. Initiatives that do not dissolve into the lifeblood of a school make no long term difference. And it requires vigilance, to stop new ways of working from being eroded and subverted by old habits.

Let me close this chapter with a cautionary tale, concerning something called 'assessment for learning' (AfL). This is an extremely well-researched set of shifts to classroom practice that produce impressive improvements in students' examination results. These shifts include teachers sharing and discussing the criteria for success with students, waiting longer for answers to questions, asking more open-ended questions, and getting students to mark their own and each others' work. These not-very-radical practices can be implemented by any teacher, with a bit of coaching. AfL's core idea is that teachers pay closer attention to students' achievements, questions and difficulties, so that they, the teachers, can diagnose difficulties and thus make their teaching better targeted and more effective. It stresses kinds of 'assessment' that are very informative for the teacher, as well as exercising 'quality control' over the students.

Sadly, once some politicians got hold of this sensible idea, they bent it out of shape, so it became a justification for ever more surveillance of learning, and even more detailed record-keeping about every child. Sadly also, although the spirit of AfL chimes very well with the Learning Gym and the Exploratory, it has overwhelmingly been used merely to improve exam results, and very little as a way of helping young people develop those portable attitudes and habits of learning. Another potentially very positive innovation has failed to escape from the gravitational field of traditional aims and familiar methods. It is this kind of subversion that a real education for life has to escape.[155]

9

How can parents help?

For education, simply, is a facet
Of childhood preparation for the lives
Children are born to lead;
It must walk hand in hand
With what they learn within their families

William, seventeen

Cultivating learning characters is not just a job for schools. It starts and continues in the home. Parenting is crucial – though all is not lost if children do come to school with some bad learning habits, or weak, undeveloped learning muscles. There are four-year-olds who arrive at school already convinced that it is their over-riding job to impress, rather than to learn. Even some toddlers have been socialised into believing that 'looking good' and 'performing well' are more important than exploring and experimenting. A group of four-year-olds were asked how they felt about making mistakes. Martin said defiantly, 'I never make mistakes.' Susie said, 'I don't do anything that's really hard.' Trevor simply advised, 'If you make a mistake you should just leave it.' But those defeatist habits can be altered at school, and they can be altered at home too.[156]

The simple, profound idea that a learning character can be cultivated applies across the lifespan. It applies to us, as well as our children. We too can benefit from signing up for the Learning Gym: making more interesting mistakes, asking deeper questions and trying things out more ingeniously. Just like our kids, we can learn to be more imaginative, more thoughtful, more empathic, more resilient and better at dealing with the changes life brings. Even with a secure pension and loving, healthy children and grandchildren, life still demands we be learners. Indeed, if all our problems were magically solved in the morning, by afternoon we would have created more. We are learning creatures through and through. So let us be the best explorers and adventurers we can be – for our own sake as much as for our children's.

Parents as models and guides of learning

Let us look at ourselves as parents first. Most fundamentally, parents need to be confident explorers around their children because their habits are contagious. Children primarily pick up their learning attitudes and habits from what they see around them at home. Characteristics, as we have seen, are easily passed on from person to person. Kurt Vonnegut's dedication to his novel *Mother Night* says: 'We are what we pretend to be, so we must be careful what we pretend to be.'[157] And nowhere is that care more vital than around our children. If parents are open-minded and inquisitive, the chances are that those traits will rub off on their children. If the family debates interesting subjects round the dinner table, and people listen to each other respectfully, and disagree graciously, then younger brothers and sisters, voracious voyeurs and eavesdroppers that they are, will pick up those habits too.

The seeds of eminent careers have been sown in just this way. At a conference I ran in 2005, Baroness Estelle Morris, a former Secretary of State for Education, and science professor Lord Robert Winston both described how, as young children, they learned the habits of debate at family meal-times. Watching and listening carefully, they served powerful apprenticeships in the arts of argument and discussion: how to take turns; how to hold their ground and when to give way; how to weave the strands of people's different contributions together. They learned what attention and respect looked and sounded like, and, little by little, these habits became absorbed into their own social miens. They learned the cadences of thoughtfulness: the acceptability of lulls and pauses in the conversation while people thought. They picked up the structures of an argument: how evidence was used, and the occasional appeal to authority. They got used to someone popping up to get a dictionary or an encyclopedia to gain clarification in the middle of the meal, and learned to treat that as normal. They began to make their own contributions, and saw that these were also listened to and respected – and gently guided sometimes, too. As they gained status and confidence, so the challenges to their own assertions became more robust, and they learned the finer skills of defence and parry and counter-charge.

Debate gave their elders satisfaction, and they saw that too. So they learned over time not just to take part in discussions, but to enjoy them. In Estelle Morris's case, the sapling of this young inclination slowly bent towards politics and the kind of debate that led to the honing of moral positions and the translation of these into policies and practices. In Robert Winston's case, a similar shoot of character grew instead in the direction of scientific inquiry: the weighing of empirical evidence, and the designing of experiments to test ideas and reveal possibilities. Different professions called, but to this day they both revel not so much in the transient security of knowing (though that has its pleasures too), but in the thrill of the intellectual chase; in the process of making new knowledge and shaping new possibilities through communal inquiry and debate. Their appetites and capacities to learn were formed and nurtured round those dining-tables because, whether wittingly or not, certain learning habits were repeatedly displayed and modelled by those they loved and admired.

Another telling example of the power of parental modelling comes from the work of American poet and academic Anne McCrary Sullivan. Sullivan wrote an essay in 2000 intriguingly entitled 'Notes from a marine biologist's daughter: on the art and science of attention'. She describes, in both poetry and prose, how, as a little girl, she served an intense apprenticeship in the habit and pleasure of simply paying detailed attention to things, as she accompanied her scientist mother.[158] In one of her poems called 'Mother collecting marine specimens' she recalls an occasion when they were both in a small skiff on

an inlet that ran under a road bridge, her mother gathering samples
from the encrusted pilings:

> In a cave-like cool, she nudges
> Grey clusters, crusty forms.
> She scrapes, selects,
> Lays silty bits and clumps
> In a bucket of clear water.
> Intent, she peers and plucks.
> A streak of blood appears on her thumb.
> She doesn't notice. She never does.
> I slide a finger over creosote blisters,
> Hear them pop, feel them flatten . . .

Here is the child ardently noticing what her mother notices – and does
not notice. She is attending a masterclass in absorption, and observing
how even a cut thumb can becomes invisible and insensible, eclipsed
by a concentration that is completely elsewhere. And the child is also
practising her own attentiveness and experimentation. The child's
borrowed fascination enables us, too, to hear those tiny explosions,
and feel the changing sensations in our fingertips as those blisters burst
and sag. As readers we can feel the poet's attention rubbing off on us,
as her mother's did on her.

In her prose reflections on these experiences, Sullivan writes:

> My mother, the scientist, taught me to see. She taught me atten-
> tion to the complexities of surface detail, and also attention to
> what lies beneath those surfaces . . . In doing so, she made me a
> poet. My mother, the teacher, held classes in mud and water and
> light. She taught with buckets and shovels and nets. Her students'
> tennis shoes squished loudly as they worked, discovered, learned.
> I observed that my mother and her students were happy. I became
> a teacher. My mother, the researcher, sat patiently at the micro-
> scope on the kitchen table, observing, noticing, discovering pat-
> terns, making sense. In that kitchen, I learned the patience of
> research. My mother was making order of the raggedness of the
> living world, and I was paying attention. But I didn't know at the
> time that I was, and I'm quite sure she didn't think that I was.

As that little girl hangs around, apparently bored perhaps, swinging her legs, idly popping creosote blisters or playing with the cat, she is also soaking up her mother's habits and pleasures in learning. She is osmosing the deep idea that learning – hard, patient, detailed, long-drawn-out learning – is both exciting and utterly absorbing. She is watching the slow process of sucking meaning out of experience, and learning that making deep sense of things, looking patiently for what is hidden, is both possible and joyous. The domains of poetry and science seem far apart; but they share this common, communicable root: the refinement of attention.

So as our children spend time with us, what do they see? What contagious attitudes and beliefs are we unwittingly transmitting? And can we recognise that our casual demonstrations of learning are as precious as the time spent helping with sums and reading – and thus determine to become more potent and benign models? Like the teachers in the last chapter, can we take pleasure in saying 'I don't know' and 'let's find out'? Do we let them see us getting frustrated – but sticking with it? Do we show them that *our* learning is sometimes hard, that we sometimes get perplexed, but we recover? Do we demonstrate that sometimes you need to walk away and cool down, and that 'leaving it for a bit' is entirely intelligent and productive? And do we see that allowing them these small glimpses of our learning attitudes is a positive contribution to their development? Can we create our own versions of those family meal-times, modelling and coaching the art of conversation?

Learning stories and family life

One useful thing for parents to do, as their children grow up, is to take them behind the scenes of family life and show them – and involve them more in – the kinds of uncertainties and challenges that inevitably exist. It is probably good to let children take the lead in this, or at least indicate what they might be interested in knowing more about – the finances, the health issues, the complicated decisions about how 'green' to be, and so on. Some young people will be ready and eager for such involvement sooner than others. But it would be good to be on the lookout for ways of sharing more of the responsibilities and complexities than the traditional family might have thought proper, not just so they can begin to learn what these issues are, but so they can use them as fruitful puzzles for developing their learning power. For instance they can begin to learn how groups work best as they help to wrestle with hard decisions. They can see what roles they can already play, and what they have yet to master.

And parents could also seize more opportunities, to tell their children – and their nieces, nephews and grandchildren – tales of their own learning journeys, warts and all, and show them that even Granddad in his prime made mistakes and found things confusing. One school in Wales that I have worked with encouraged parents to share their difficulties with reading, writing and spelling with their children: to talk together about how they faced such learning difficulties, and to explore what can be done to get over the hurdles they meet. What the school was trying to do was not just to help the children spell better, but to think about how they could become better *learners of spelling*, and to recruit parents in this task. Parents and children together came up with a variety of ingenious ways in which they could all learn more powerfully – and as a result, the children's spelling started to improve faster than traditional methods of teaching had managed to achieve. And both children and parents said it was more fun, and less slog.[159]

How should parents respond when their child is getting stuck and making mistakes? One of the things that parents sometimes do wrong, from a learning point of view, is prematurely rescuing their children from learning challenges. As we have seen, it is not difficulty per se that upsets young learners. Babies are incredibly resilient in the face of complicated things, like learning to walk, that take weeks or months even to begin to master. They don't worry about looking stupid; they want to learn to walk, and if that takes falling over dozens of times a day, then they will fall down – and get up and try again. The problem comes if we inadvertently lead children to believe that mistakes are something that it is right to get upset about.

If we rush in at the first sign of frustration, and scoop up a toddler, stroke her tenderly, and say 'there, there, never mind', we are teaching her that there is indeed something to mind about – and that she *needed* to be rescued. By being over-solicitous, we might even be transmitting *our* discomfort with mistakes, and thus making her a less resilient learner, quicker to give up and less willing to risk something that she does not already know how to do. Of course kids sometimes need rescuing from real danger. But we can help their learning power grow by sometimes restraining the impulse to comfort and reassure.[160] There is nothing worse than being constantly hovered over by an anxious supervisor, whether you are three or forty-three. And the awareness of that anxious presence acts as a potent distraction, so you are less able to give your full attention to the challenge at hand – so, in a kind of vicious spiral, you end up making more mistakes and needing more help than you would if you had been left alone.

We may also need to restrain our enthusiasm to teach. Children are extremely good at learning what they need to know, at that moment, in order to get on with the project in hand, whatever that is. Their learning operates best on a 'just in time' basis. They are not so good at learning things 'just in case' it might come in handy sometime in the future. Many adults, on the other hand, love to teach and explain, and can take a simple request for help as an opening for a fifteen minute lecture. You probably know the old story of the little girl who asked her mother how traffic lights worked. 'Sorry, sweetie, I'm busy,' she said 'Why don't you go and ask your father.' 'Oh no,' said the child, 'I don't want to know *that* much about it.' When kids get stuck, what they usually want is the *least* help that will get them going again, and they can fiercely resent being helped too much.

If you want your child to grow up a confident, capable learner, increasingly allow *them* to dictate when they need help, and what kind of help they need. And if they are doing fine, don't interrupt them and try to get them to talk about what they are doing, or 'trying to do'. Having to explain yourself can badly disrupt the kind of valuable non-verbal learning that is going on, and it is often of no value, other than to assuage an adult's idle curiosity. Indeed, much of the most interesting and imaginative learning occurs when you don't really know what you are trying to achieve, and you have no clear plan to follow. You are just 'messing about', seeing how stuff behaves, discovering what you can do with sand or GarageBand software.

The perils of praise

Parents should be careful how much praise and encouragement they give. Powerful learners don't need much encouragement; they are learning because they want to. Paradoxically, children who are praised all the time become less creative and imaginative, and they become less confident to learn on their own. It is as if they become addicted to the continual stream of praise and approval, so that when it doesn't happen they are thrown. They have learned to learn for the approval, not for the intrinsic pleasure and purpose of getting better at something. The same thing has been shown to happen with real rewards and incentives. If you pay a child for engaging in an activity they enjoy anyway, and you later stop the rewards, you will find that the enjoyment has disappeared, and they no longer engage 'just for its own sake'. The external reward has killed their intrinsic satisfaction.[161]

There is one kind of praise that is particularly bad, and that is to keep telling children they are clever, intelligent or talented. If you feel you must keep up the stream of encouraging noises, praise the effort they put in, not how 'smart' they must be. As we saw in chapter 4, such praise is effectively teaching children that there are two kinds of things in the world: things they are naturally good at, and therefore find relatively easy, and things they are not cut out for, which they find hard. The net effect of this is to make them stop trying if they can't immediately do something.

Young people who are consistently told they are 'bright' or 'talented' adopt lower standards of success, become conservative in the degrees of challenge they will engage with, under-rate the importance of effort in learning, and turn to a parent or teacher for help the minute they get stuck. Being trained to attribute success to 'ability', and lack of success to 'lack of ability', directly and significantly weakens their learning spirit. This applies as much at home as it does in school. Comment on your children's effort and tenacity, and they will come to enjoy harder and harder challenges. Praise them for their ability, and they will become more timid and cautious.[162] For parents with a mistaken belief in the fragility of 'self-esteem' this can sound like strange advice. But a weight of research evidence is on my side. It is worth trying to shift the habit of telling children what they are and are not 'good at'. And when you do praise your children, keep it sparing, keep it specific and keep it real. Don't do it too often. And when you do, make sure it applies to something that really deserves praise. Bland, non-specific, unearned praise does not build 'self-esteem'; it just makes children doubt your judgement, and learn to disregard whatever you say.

Even informal remarks about a child's achievements at school can transmit these dangerous mental viruses. Jacquelynne Eccles at the University of Michigan has studied how parents respond to their children's school reports. Their reactions turn out to depend both on the subject and the gender of the child. In maths, boys who have done well tend to be told it must be because they are 'good at it', while poor performance is more often taken to reflect a lack of effort. For girls on the other hand, good marks receive an 'effort attribution' – 'You must have really tried hard' – while low marks are taken to suggest a lack of ability. The net effect of this is that boys tend to improve more – because 'effort' is something you can increase – while girls tend to plateau, because 'ability' is assumed to be fixed. Interestingly, in English the pattern is reversed. Girls are told they do well because they are 'bright' and badly because they were 'lazy'. Boys do well because they tried and badly because they 'aren't good at it'. The moral of the story? First, be careful about the stories you tell your children. It is safer to ask them for their explanations than it is to presume that you know the cause yourself. And second, be sceptical about the media. Eccles found that parents' tendency to purvey these stereotyped theories to their children reflected their uncritical exposure to those ideas in television shows and magazines.[163]

Strong walls for the home Exploratory

If we go right back to basics, what children need, to grow their learning power, is a home with safe and clear boundaries and routines within which they can find for themselves plenty of interesting challenges to engage with – and then be left, within the bounds of safety, to get on with it. Especially with young children, that framework of clear and consistent routines and expectations turns out to be vital. Mothers who 'set the limits' and stick to them produce children who are more resilient and robust in the face of uncertainty than those who are more laissez-faire or inconsistent. This research even shows that 'insisting on being obeyed', and rating 'obedience' as an important trait to cultivate, are maternal attitudes that breed adventurous children. It is as if a clear ring around children frees them up to explore, knowing that nothing too bad can happen; whereas if there are holes in the (literal or metaphorical) fence that you can crawl through, and nobody will notice or care, your world is insecure, and you learn to be more cautious. Of course, as children grow up, so the boundaries are pushed back and become less rigid – but if that happens too soon, that vital sense that the world is safe enough to explore, and that exploration usually pays off, may be jeopardised, and their learning becomes stunted and brittle.[164]

Within that expanding haven, make sure there is plenty of general-purpose stuff to play with and explore. You do not need to buy loads of expensive 'educational toys', the justification for which is often extremely dubious. The more open-ended the play-potential of a toy is, the more it allows the child to use and stretch their imagination. The more glossy and purpose-built, the more likely it is to prescribe and limit the ways in which it can be used, and the less opportunity for creativity it affords. And children do not need to be over-stimulated. They do not need, nor benefit from, an endless array of sights, sounds, touches and smells. Such a diet of strong stimulation may merely have the effect of creating an expectation for it – a kind of habituation that can border on an addiction – so they become less tolerant of situations that are slow and quiet, and thus less able to find amusement and exploration in wet bubbles of creosote, or whatever.

Imagination is the child of boredom, so allowing your child to discover that being bored isn't so bad, to tolerate the quiet times, and to learn to use their own imagination to 'rescue' themselves from boredom, is a useful regime for your child. Powerful learners have to know how to find and create the right kinds of challenge for themselves, and continually being fed challenges, however interesting they may be, will not strengthen their ability to nose out and develop learning challenges of their own.

It has been suggested that one of the effects of television, especially children's cartoons, if watched too much, can be the creation of such an acquired need for stimulation, with the concomitant inability to tolerate environments – like many classrooms – where the learning on offer is less 'zappy and grabby'. Habituation to the intense stimulation of television also makes the kind of sustained attention that reading requires harder, so children do less of it, so they fail to learn both the skills of reading and its pleasures.[165]

The internet can be like that too. It can be used to feed the surfing-for-stimulation habit, or it can be used to learn how to scuba-dive for deeper information and ideas. Both are useful, and satisfying: it isn't either/or unless we forget to boost one or other of them. There is no reason why idly surfing a website, or playing fast-moving action games, should prevent children from also learning the skills and pleasures of slower, deeper kinds of learning and attention. Both are good. My advice to parents is to model both, and to exercise a little light 'parental guidance', so that both agility and stamina of mind are developed side by side. Use the computer for challenges that require patient thinking and reading, as well for those that build rapid hand-eye coordination. There are games and activities for both, so make sure it is part of family life to use them both.

Having said that, parents should not feel they have to create the Perfect Learning Environment for their children. Children's developing brains are so complicated that we simply cannot know what they might be ready and keen to learn 'next'. Much better to have a rough guess as to what might interest them, and then sit back and watch. Your guess may be wide of the mark, and the play-possibilities either too easy or too hard. If that is the case you will soon find out. It is much more likely that your children will find some way of making use of your offering for themselves that may be quite different from what you imagined, but will be entirely appropriate to their needs. And if they ask for a bit of help in customising the situation so they can get a juicy challenge out of it, by all means respond. But make sure you are following where they are going (provided the real risks are not too great), and resisting the urge to think you know better.

Language and questions

The language we use at home is as important as that used at school. Parents should remember to use the language of learning. When children come home from school, we can do better than to ask 'How was school?' (and being ritually told 'OK' or 'Boring'). We can ask:

- What was hard for you today?
- Which learning muscles have you been stretching?
- Did you ask a good question?
- Did you risk tackling something new?
- What did you manage to improve?
- Did you make any interesting mistakes?
- Did you learn anything useful by watching someone else?
- How could you have helped your teacher get that tricky stuff across better?
- How would you have organised the lesson differently?

Any such questions can open up thoughtful conversations about the process of learning (and teaching), and help young people absorb the idea that learning is something to be thought and talked about, and something at which we can all get better.

Parents' pester power: talk to the school about your child's learning

When children go to school, parents need to watch carefully to see if the children's learning power is expanding or contracting. Is the school the kind of place that is making children more curious or less; more willing to risk and explore, or more timid and conservative; more imaginative and better thinkers, or more passive retainers of what they have been told; more collaborative and empathic, or more competitive and individualistic in their learning? It is good for parents to talk to their children's teachers about the ways in which they are developing their children's ability to cope well with real-life challenges. And if they have never thought of education like that, it will do no harm for parents to press for answers.

Here are ten good questions to ask your child's teacher:

1. What have you noticed about my child as a learner outside lessons? How much do you know about my child's interests?
2. What are you trying to capture in the way you write reports about my child? How do you know if you are being successful? When will you ask for my feedback about the way reports on my child are written?
3. Is there a good spirit of learning in the staffroom? Do teachers ask and offer help to get better at their jobs? Do staff mainly talk about learning, or about troublemakers, at coffee time?
4. Do you value education as a preparation for lifelong learning? How have you demonstrated this value to the pupils today?
5. How do you demonstrate to my child and me what you genuinely value more than exams and good behaviour?
6. How do you encourage children's curiosity outside the set curriculum?
7. Is PE more about winning or learning? How much do pupils design their own coaching?
8. How much real responsibility do my children have to choose what, when and how they are learning? How much part do pupils play in determining the core business of the school?
9. How much opportunity does my child get to help teachers improve their teaching?
10. How do you check whether your intention to help children become better learners is being realised? What do you know about the lives of your past students after they have left your school?

Families as learning communities

As parents, we are responsible for creating a positive learning environment for our children. But being a parent is itself a huge learning challenge. Most parents these days spend a large amount of their time in the Don't Know Zone. So it is for their own sake, as much as for their children's, that parents need to pay attention to their own learning fitness, and learn to become more and more comfortable in the readymade Exploratory that their home inevitably is. As children grow up, so the challenges they present to their parents change, but there are few parents lucky enough to spend more than short periods in the quiet still waters of stability and harmony. From the learning rapids of the new baby to the anxieties over whether their toddler is meeting the 'developmental milestones'; from bullying at school to the stress of exams; from adolescence to the different challenges when the kids leave home: family life is a learning jungle.

So parents who are trying to develop their own learning characters are achieving two goals at once: they are improving their own lives, and they are providing better models for their children. They create their family culture so that it reminds them to be good team players; to listen carefully and check understanding; to brainstorm possibilities, and to analyse them; to stick with hard stuff, and give challenges and decisions the time they need; to balance clear structure with freedom and playfulness; to help all concerned acknowledge that sometimes learning is hard or confusing. Pre-emptive conversational strikes and verbal rail-roading (by any family member) should fall away as everyone learns to be collectively more vigilant about the times when learning can be hijacked by premature certainty.

Think about ways of opening the family to learning, employing techniques to keep the questioning going and taking opportunities to turn one person's 'job' into a whole family project. There may be a board in the kitchen where family members post on-going questions. There may be family forums about 'how we could manage X or Y better'. Planning the next family holiday can become a collaborative project, in which everyone can be both researcher and advocate. Parents can take opportunities to talk about their own professional challenges and uncertainties, gradually peeling away any veneer of omniscience to reveal their own learning feelings and processes.

In a complicated, fast-changing world the intelligent path is to let go of being a Knower and embrace being a Learner. And we should create organisations, whether they be families, offices or schools, where Learning is routinely valued over Knowing. We must all, adults as much as young people, stay open and flexible, 'expect the unexpected', and keep learning. The heroes of today are not those who love to display their knowledge, but those who are virtuoso investigators, questioners and problem-solvers. The new sciences of learning, with their demonstrations of all the ways in which learning power can be stretched and amplified, are good news for adults as well as for young people. We now know that older dogs *can* learn new tricks – and we should embrace the promise this opens up for us.

TIPS FOR RAISING LEARNERS

- Be a visible learner for your children
- Involve children in adult conversations
- Let them spend time with you while you are doing difficult things
- Involve children in family decisions
- Tell your children stories about your learning difficulties
- Encourage children to spend time with people who have interesting things to share
- Don't rush in too quickly to rescue children when they are having difficulties
- Restrain the impulse to teach
- Don't praise too much – use interest rather than approval
- Acknowledge the effort, not the 'ability'
- Make clear boundaries and maintain them
- Don't over stimulate – boredom breeds imagination
- Choose multi-purpose and open-ended toys
- Encourage different kinds of computer use
- Talk to children about the process of learning (without offering too much advice)
- Watch and learn from your children's learning

10

Bringing learning to life: rediscovering the heart of education

> There are good people who hold this information [about global warming] at arms' length, because if they acknowledge it, the moral imperative to make changes becomes inescapable.
>
> Al Gore, *An Inconvenient Truth*

Schools must change. The case is overwhelming. It is education's core responsibility to prepare young people for the future, and it is failing in that duty. As things stand, less than half of all young people go on to university, and many of those who do, now endure an assembly-line experience at least as passive and depersonalised as school. The 'less fortunate' majority go out into the world bemused by an eleven year experience that they were told was of massive importance, but whose net effect has been to leave many of them with a smattering of certificates, and a strong feeling of not having been adequately prepared for the rigours and complexities of real life.

In the preceding chapters, we have reviewed the research that shows that many young people, the 'successes' as well as the 'failures', feel less confident, less resilient, less capable of meeting unforeseen challenges, than they did when they were young children. We now know that it is both scientifically credible, and educationally feasible, to attend more successfully to cultivating the qualities of character and mind that modern life demands: determination, curiosity, imagination, disciplined thinking, a love of genuine debate, scepticism. New research brings us the encouraging news that minds are indeed malleable. They are more expandable than they are fixed. Intelligence is not a hereditary life sentence; it is a multi-faceted resource whose many aspects can be cultivated.

We already have many examples and much evidence of the success of this way of running schools. Boys struggling with maths improve dramatically when they have just an hour a week, for six weeks, to sit and talk about how they learn (and no extra maths-specific tuition). GCSE results improve when teachers start thinking and talking about young people's learning habits, and add these observations to their reports.

The vice-chair of governors at a Wiltshire primary school has written to me about the impact she has seen of these methods on her own children:

> I have been fascinated by the impact that [learning to learn methods] have had on our children and in particular the way they have raised confidence, independence and achievement in many areas. On a personal level, I am particularly aware of this as two of my own children moved up to secondary school before these methods were introduced, and two experienced at least a few years of their impact. There is a marked difference in their approach to learning, in particular in their levels of resilience.

Walthamstow School for Girls has had a very positive Ofsted report which singled out their work with these methods. The school has joined the 13% of schools inspected in England in 2006/7 that were judged 'outstanding'. The inspectors found that 'few schools in similar contexts [a socio-economically deprived area of London] do as well as this school to prepare students so well for life'. One of the key factors in this success was judged to be their attention to the girls' learning muscles. The headteacher, Rachel MacFarlane, explained that these methods enable them to 'support [the girls] to develop a set of skills and learning dispositions they can use in their whole life, not just in school. We now know how to produce smarter, more confident learners who are able to cope with all aspects of life.'[166]

Time in the Learning Gym is, the results show, time well spent. These approaches are cheap: no expensive kit is required. Anarchy does not break out if young people are coached to organise learning for themselves. As kids become more interested in their own expandable learning capacity, Shakespeare does not go out of the window. And, at the same time as real-world confidence increases, the results go up.

If expanding young people's minds is an achievable goal, it is also a highly desirable one. More than anything, young people themselves crave the confidence to face their complicated lives. If they do not have that confidence, they and their communities are at risk. Personal well-being and social cohesion are both at stake, as is the economic competitiveness of the nation. With the confidence to learn, young men and women have more initiative, work better in teams, and are less afraid of responsibility. That is what employers keep saying they want. But they won't get these qualities till schools are redesigned so they explicitly and deliberately stretch and build them.

Despite the strength of the case for change, progress has, as we have seen, been slow. Government reforms of class size, exam structures or private financing don't work because they leave in place the things that actually need reform: the classroom ethos and methods, and the assumptions that underpin them, which I critiqued in chapters 4 and 5. Those hoary old metaphors for school, the assembly line and the monastery, and the associated beliefs about intelligence and knowledge that go with them, are surprisingly hardy. As soon as we take our eye off them, they slide back into our collective unconscious and resume their covert operations of guiding and limiting our sense of what is possible or sensible.

We can see these assumptions and prejudices at work in statements like this:

> The rot set in in the 1960s when trendy new theories began to circulate about how children should be educated. Out went the old-fashioned notion of the teacher as an authority figure whose job it is to pass on a body of useful knowledge from historical dates to times tables. In came the idea of a new child-centred style of education, placing lots more emphasis on discovery, imagination and self-esteem, and considerably less on discipline, rote-learning, competitiveness and, er, acquiring knowledge.[167]

There's no argument or inquisitiveness here. Words and phrases like 'rot', 'trendy', 'child-centred' and 'the 1960s' are used to convey the impression that the writer's position is not only common sense, but that anything else is self-evidently bonkers. This author (and others) falsely assume that you can't build the skills of discovery *and* 'pass on useful knowledge' at the same time. There's no questioning of how useful the historical dates are, nor what is to be gained and lost by dealing with them in different ways. Any such attempts at sophistication are immediately stigmatised as 'trendy nonsense'. For some, the unconscious analogies of the monastery and the assembly line are still firmly in place.

In the face of such knee-jerk thinking, we have to work hard even to make the Learning Gym and the Exploratory images seem plausible and interesting, let alone for them to become 'second nature'. From where I sit, the importance of that third perspective, of seeing school as an apprenticeship in the craft of learning, is just plain obvious. Of course the content is important, and so are the qualifications. But those two familiar perspectives do not cover everything that matters about school. However, what seems so self-evident to me can sound like claptrap to some, and if we are to make the progress that's needed, we also need to understand more fully why some people seem so resistant to new ways of thinking about education.

Tradition on their side?

There is nothing more difficult and dangerous to undertake, nor more doubtful of success, than to take the lead in the introduction of a new order of things; because the innovator has for enemies all those who have done well under the old order, and only lukewarm support from those who would do well under the new. This coolness reflects a fear of the old guard, who have tradition on their side, and also people's general suspicion of unfamiliar innovations.

Machiavelli, *The Prince*

Some resistance comes from those buried assumptions about what school *is*. But there are other sources of inertia that contribute to the slow rate of change in education, and Machiavelli puts his finger on some of them.

Education is big business, and there are armies of publishers, officials, examiners, consultants, private tutors and manufacturers of equipment whose lives might be disturbed, and livelihoods threatened, by some of the ideas in this book. (At a vast education 'expo' in Brazil recently I watched teachers from poor schools being seduced with free crayons into ordering coloured plastic desks for their dirt-floored classrooms, and an interactive whiteboard being proudly wiped clean of old-fashioned sums with a clever electronic eraser.) There will indeed be enemies amongst those who have 'done well under the old order'.

There is also political and bureaucratic inertia. The centralised control of national education by elected politicians is a recipe for disaster. In office for only a few years, fearful of doing anything to upset the electorate, yet obliged to look busy, effective and important, what else can a politician do but regularly announce fine-sounding initiatives that seem to require impressive amounts of money, but which cannot either risk or challenge too much, for fear of an adverse media reaction from journalists with their own axes to grind?

As a result, it often seems to be the job of policy-makers simply to codify changes that are already happening, a sobering – and in some ways encouraging – fact that only a few of them seem to realise. Geoff Mulgan was Tony Blair's long-time Head of Strategy at 10 Downing Street. In his recent book *Good and Bad Power* he says:

> One of the optical illusions of government is that those inside of it think of themselves as drivers of change . . . Yet most far-reaching ideas and changes come from outside . . . Most radical change has to start outside government, usually from the bottom [up] rather than the top [down] . . . New ideas need time to evolve, preferably away from the spotlight. Governments are more often vehicles than initiators. They play a role in embedding those changes, but typically they get involved only at a late stage.[168]

Because of their inherent timidity, policy-makers are always playing catch-up. For example, when DfES officials found out that lots of teachers were enthused by the idea of 'learning styles' documents suddenly started appearing from the DfES telling them what a good idea it was to take account of students' learning styles. So it will be as thousands of teachers find more and more ways of cultivating characters fit for the Learning Age. We are at the stage now where exciting ideas are evolving away from the spotlight. In ten years' time they will become 'policy' – but adventurous schools don't need to wait for such retrospective sanctioning.

Inertia also reflects, as Machiavelli noted, the numbers of people who are not natural pioneers, but need to 'wait and see', and have more evidence to be convinced. There are many teachers who do not yet believe that Learning to Learn could make a real difference for the disaffected students they have to deal with every day. Few of us welcome our long-held beliefs or our hard-won expertise being threatened. Naturally there is some scepticism. Scepticism is the open-minded attitude of the learner who is not dazzled by hype, but is open to persuasion. I don't expect teachers to take this on trust, however, any more than I would myself if I had not seen its worth proved a thousand times with my own eyes. But if we agree that young people need to be braver, subtler learners, it is surely worth trying out one or two new ideas. Learning to learn is not a miracle cure for all ills. And it is still early days. Though we know that the approach is scientifically credible, practically viable and socially desirable, there is much more that we are learning every week about how to do it better, with an increasingly wide range of children and young people. But so far, we are finding that there are a great many winners.

Amongst the faint-hearted there may also be some parents who cannot believe that school could be much different from the way it was for them. If they did well, they may simply see school as a game at which their own children are also likely to succeed, and therefore not to be tampered with. Their children will serve their time, get those four As and go to a good university. No matter that the content seems to offer little purchase on the real world, nor that their bright child is bored from 9 a.m. until 3 p.m., impatiently waiting to get back to their books, their own computer or their friends, and do something interesting at home.

It is more often when children seem miserable or rebellious, that parents begin to question what is happening at school, to take note of the yawning gulf between Lessons and Life, and to ask themselves whether school is really fit for purpose, and whether young people are really being well served. Sadly, this is happening more and more often, but the positive side is that parents can now see that there is an alternative, that school doesn't have to be the way it is and that they can, as parents, take action at home and they can also nudge schools towards change.

Students themselves can resist change – having been schooled for so long in passivity they can balk at taking any responsibility. After a term of trying to get one of his classes to take more responsibility for their learning, Australian science teacher Ian Mitchell was cornered at break by two of his most recalcitrant fourteen year olds. 'Mr Mitchell, we think we've finally figured out what it is you want us to do,' one of them said. 'Yes?' said Ian, hopefully. 'You want us to think for ourselves, don't you?' 'That's it exactly,' said Ian, sensing a breakthrough. 'Yeah, well,' said the other boy, 'we don't wanna do that.'[169]

At such moments, we can discover how resilient *we* really are. In order to win young people over, it is vital to start small and not give up. Ian Mitchell persisted, and eventually converted many young people who were sceptical or resistant to begin with. Grandiose revolutions are full of sound and fury, and it is all too easy to lose momentum, after the initial fanfare, and for young people, as well as their teachers, to find that they fizzle out and signify not very much. That's why the revolution I am advocating starts small, is sustained, and comes to seep into the fabric of a school, so that the implicit sense of purpose shifts coherently, pervasively – and irreversibly.

What is needed to overcome the resistances to the requisite reform is not more changes to structures and procedures. It is an upsurge of will and imagination amongst large numbers of parents and teachers. If enough people are clear about what *must* be done, if enough teachers see how much *can* be done, if the officials begin to see that students really are becoming more robust, resilient and resourceful in their attitude to life, and if exam results actually improve, then the policymakers will, as Geoff Mulgan says, start drafting documents that suggest what a good idea it would be if people did exactly what the more adventurous are already doing.

Beware false prophets

Tinkering with the curriculum and examinations regime will not lead to a sustained culture change, and neither, I am convinced, will any form of quick fix. As we saw in chapter 3, changes such as allowing children to drink water in class, or using 'brain gym' techniques have no deep effects – although they cause no harm. The jury is still out on the cognitive effects of fish oils. There are drugs appearing that claim to be 'cognitive enhancers', but their long-term efficacy and effects remain unproven. If we want all young people to become more confident and capable learners in real-life, there is, as yet, no magic bullet, pharmaceutical or otherwise.

Information and communication technology (ICT) has also been hailed as an educational saviour. Electronic technologies do indeed hold a great deal of promise for the development of education, but we must be sure we do not lapse into blind faith in computers, any more than in fish oils. Millions of pounds have been spent on supplying schools with computers, but a good many machines lie idle, or perform only menial tasks like taking the register. Interactive whiteboards can be used as tools to stretch young people's imaginations, or they can be used merely as a snazzy blackboard. Young people can use computers in ways that build their powers of collaboration and innovation, but I have also seen students sitting in front of a screen doing exactly the same kinds of tedious busywork that I was getting from a textbook in the 1950s.

Not all young people conform to the stereotype of the geeky 'cyberkid', but most of them are very comfortable with digital technologies. They tend to be highly effective learners both in the mastery of these technologies, and in they way they use them – with little or no formal tuition. Young people's learning often gets launched by elder siblings and parents, but then develops through informal chat with friends and contacts, and trial and error. Many young people are much more savvy and discerning about their use of Google and Wikipedia than adults fear. They know that some games 'turn your brain to mush' while others really make you think in hard and exciting ways. However, they may be less sceptical in their internet use than they could be. Hannah Green and Celia Hannon in a recent Demos report have shown how schools could play a more powerful role, not in co-opting and corralling young people's IT explorations, but in helping them develop the kind of reflective awareness that builds discernment and transfer.[170] As we have seen, young people have a portfolio of learning techniques of their own which ICT can help to develop further. They choose their own challenges and set their own – often very high – standards. They exchange knowledge and ideas freely and, in doing so, are stretching and strengthening sophisticated skills of collaboration and knowledge-sharing. MSN and Internet Relay Chat, while they have potential for abuse, make it very easy to find friends who are into the same things as you, regardless of distance. Young people love creative tinkering, either alone or together, but without any authority looking over their shoulders to make sure they are doing it 'right'. And they are motivated by the challenge of producing a product or a performance that they can submit to critical appraisal, and hopefully acclaim, by a selected jury of their peers. Creating your own playlist with iTunes, posting your photographs on Flickr, building a website for yourself or your friends: such projects greatly extend the portfolio of real challenges that are there for them to choose from. In the context of such interesting challenges, school seems to many young people merely an irrelevance or an irritation.

But there is an important distinction between the effects *with*, and the effects *of*, technology. *With* a computer, you can do all sorts of things that you couldn't do without, just as you can with a bike or a TV. You can go to more places and see more things. But there is a lingering question about what the long-term effects *of* using that technology are. A bike-ride gets you somewhere, but it also helps general fitness. A motorbike takes you further, but doesn't work your muscles at the same time. The lasting effects of different technologies vary greatly, and depend not just on what the technology is, but how you are using it. Are you becoming more thoughtful, resourceful, resilient and intelligent, as you work with the tool? Or are you becoming more lazy, passive and dependent? This is where the mediation of the teacher, and the awareness of the learner, are crucial. When I run a spell-check, I can run it mindlessly, simply pressing a key to replace the wrong word with the right one without really thinking. Or I can look and think and try to learn and improve. It depends entirely on my intention and the frame of mind I bring to the activity. Machines by themselves do not deliver education.

Another suggestion for renewing education is that it should directly aim to teach happiness. Lord Richard Layard of the London School of Economics has been a forceful champion of this idea. He adopts a very similar starting point to mine: many young people are stressed and unhappy, and that this is an issue for educators as much as for politicians, therapists and youth workers. But Layard's solution is different: he thinks we should make 'happiness' into a new school subject. As he rightly says, we know a good deal from current psychology about what makes people happy and unhappy. Good summaries of this research are to be found in books such as Jonathan Haidt's *The Happiness Hypothesis*, and Layard's own *Happiness: Lessons from a New Science*. Layard thinks this knowledge should be communicated to young people in courses on 'life skills' (a souped-up version of Personal, Social and Health Education, PSHE). The curriculum should include topics like 'managing your feelings', 'loving and serving others' and 'appreciating beauty'.[171]

The intentions behind these proposals are clearly good, but I doubt that lessons on 'emotional intelligence' and 'serving others' will do the deep work that is needed. Knowledge of the risks of smoking does not stop people doing it, and I have no confidence that knowledge of what makes us happier will change the dysfunctional habits by which so many of us, adults as well as young people, contrive to subvert our own happiness.

Happiness is better seen as a regular by-product of having done something challenging and worthwhile. Happiness is a mixture of pride, satisfaction and the sense of effectiveness and value that arises when we have stretched ourselves to achieve something we care about. In other words, happiness is the fruit of worthwhile learning. In my view, too much stress and unhappiness in young people's lives comes from the fact that they do not know how to learn, nor what it is that they want to learn about. If we can help them to discover the things they most passionately want to get better at, and to develop the confidence and capability to pursue those passions, then I think more happiness and less stress will be the result.

The next step

I hope this book will inspire people to help their students and children become brave and confident explorers, tough enough in spirit, and flexible enough in mind, to pursue their dreams and ambitions. In the Learning Gym, young people learn by doing. There is time and opportunity to gradually build up their learning muscles. There are teacher-coaches who help to personalise learning, so that young people grow in independence and imagination. There are teams of co-explorers who encourage one another, applaud each other's progress and share ideas and resources. Everyone speaks the language of learning, because it seeps into the way people think about themselves, until 'being a learner' becomes a core part of their character and identity. If we want young people to be entrepreneurial, we shouldn't teach them about setting up small businesses and managing accounts, we should coach them to be bold and inquisitive, resilient and resourceful, creative and collaborative.

We need a new narrative for education that can engage and inspire children and their families – a tale of trials and adventure, of learning derring-do and learning heroism. Let us fire kids up with the deep satisfaction of discovery and exploration. They are born with learning zeal; let us recognise, celebrate and protect it, but also stretch, strengthen and diversify it.

Endnotes

1. John Dewey, *Education and Experience*, 1938, p. 26.
2. Samantha Parsons and John Bynner, *Does Numeracy Matter More?* National Research and Development Centre, Institute of Education, 2005.3.
3. James T. Dillon, *The Practice of Questioning*, Routledge: London, 1990.
4. Chris Whetton, Graham Ruddock and Liz Twist, 'Standards in English primary education: the international evidence', *Primary Review Research Briefings*, 4/2, University of Cambridge, 2007.
5. Stephan Collishaw, Barbara Maughan, Robert Goodman and Andrew Pickles, 'Time trends in adolescent mental health', *Journal of Child Psychology and Psychiatry*, 2004, 45(8), pp. 1350–62.
6. Reported in 'Doubt and depression burden teenage girls', *The Guardian*, 24/2/05.
7. 'Pupils' alcohol drinking: behaviour, influences and consequences', *Young People Now/The Office of the Children's Commissioner*, London, July 2006.
8. 'British children: poorer, at greater risk and more insecure', *The Guardian* 15/2/07.
9. See Collishaw et al., 'Time trends in adolescent mental health'.
10. *Truth Hurts: Report of the National Inquiry into Self-harm among Young People*, Mental Health Foundation, 2006.
11. 'Teenagers' self-harm', Mental Health Foundation report, 27 March 2006; reported in 'Teenagers' epidemic of self-harm', *Observer* 26/3/06.
12. Reported in 'A leap into danger', *The Guardian* 3/7/06.
13. Comment on Collishaw et al. report, 'Today's youth: anxious, depressed, anti-social', *The Guardian* 13/10/04.

14. James Crinson and John Williamson, 'Non-standard dialect in the formal speech of 15-year-olds on Tyneside', *Language and Education*, 2004,
18(3), pp. 207–19. Andrew Smith, 'Where did you find that voice?' *The
Observer*, 12/3/2000.
15. David Hicks, *Lessons for the Future: The Missing Dimension in Education*,
RoutledgeFalmer: London, 2002.
16. Retrieved from childline.org.uk, 23/11/07.
17. Reported in 'Exam strain on schools "too great"', *The Observer*, 26/3/06.
18. Quoted in 'Walking back to happiness', *The Guardian* 20/3/07.
19. In November 2007 I ran a workshop for a mixture of primary and secondary students and their teachers to explore these worries, and these
were the ones that came out top.
20. This summary alludes to an important book by Robert Kegan called *In
Over Our Heads: The Mental Demands of Modern Life*, Harvard
University Press: Cambridge MA, 1995.
21. Jonathan Haidt, *The Happiness Hypothesis*, William Heinemann:
London, 2006, p. 221.
22. We'll come back to look at these alternatives in a little more detail in
chapter 10.
23. J. C. Chapman and G. S. Counts, *Principles of Education*, Houghton
Mifflin: Boston,1924.
24. Actually, there are exceptions to this. There was a time when Intel found
it cheaper to reject half of all the chips they produced, than to improve
the quality of the production line. Silicone, however, is very much
cheaper than flesh and blood.
25. 'Illiterate pupils cost £10bn a year, warn businesses', *The Independent*,
21/8/06.
26. Survey of truanting in London by Smart Technologies, reported in
'Report says a quarter of pupils play truant', *The Guardian*, 6/2/06; 'So
why aren't you in school, then', *The Independent* 5/10/06.
27. Rebecca Clarkson and Marian Sainsbury, *Children's Attitudes to Reading*,
NFER, 2007.
28. These results are summarised by Bethan Marshall, Children are not
helped by reading too early, *The Independent*, 6/12/07. For the original
PIRLS research reports, see *http://timss.bc.edu/pirls2006*.
29. Ruth Deakin-Crick, Patricia Broadfoot and Guy Claxton, 'Developing
an effective lifelong learning inventory: The ELLI project', *Assessment in
Education*, 2004, 11(3), pp. 247–72. Ruth Deakin-Crick, Barbara

McCombs, Alice Haddon, Patricia Broadfoot and Marilyn Tew, 'The ecology of learning: factors contributing to learner-centred classroom cultures', *Research Papers in Education*, 2007, 22(3), pp. 267–307.

30. New Economics Foundation report, *The Guardian* 27/4/04.

31. Carol Dweck, *Self-theories: Their Role in Motivation, Personality and Development*, Psychology Press: London, 1999.

32. Quoted in David Perkins, *Outsmarting IQ: The Emerging Science of Learnable Intelligence*, Free Press, 1995.

33. David Hargreaves, *About Learning: Report of the Learning Working Group*, Demos: London, 2004.

34. Cited in Richard Aldrich, *An Introduction to the History of Education*, Hodder and Stoughton: London, 1982.

35. Ron Ritchhart, *Intellectual Character: What It Is, Why It Matters, And How to Get It*, Jossey-Bass, San Francisco, 2002, pp. 8–9.

36. This list was generated by people at a meeting convened by the UK Government's Chief Scientist to discuss 'Mental Capacity and Well-being for the 21st Century', London, April 2007.

37. This list was generated by the 1500 international delegates at the 13th International Conference on Thinking in Sweden, June 2007. At one point we were all asked to post on a long wall our thoughts about what would be contained in a 'Curriculum for the Unknown'. In other words, what did we think children would need in order to cope with a non-traditional, unpredictable world. As I scanned the Post-Its, several elements of this new 'core curriculum' stood out.

38. See *www.education-otherwise.org*.

39. See Noel Entwistle, *Styles of Learning and Teaching*, Beekman Books: Wappingers Falls NY, 1990; Jo Boaler, 'When even the winners are losers: evaluating the experience of "top set" students', *Journal of Curriculum Studies*, 1997, 29(2), pp. 165–82.

40. Phil Mullan, 'Education – it's not for the economy, stupid!' *www.spiked-online.com*, 3 August 2004.

41. Richard Dawkins, 'Beyond belief', *The Guardian*, 10/1/06.

42. Dylan Wiliam, 'Content then process: formative assessment in teacher learning communities', In D. B. Reeves (ed.), *Ahead of the Curve: The Power of Assessment to Transform Teaching and Learning*, Solution Tree: Bloomington IN, 2007.

43. See *www.primaryreview.org.uk*.

44. 'One in six admit to cheating', *Times Higher Education Supplement*,

17/3/06. Frank Furedi, 'What's wrong with cheats?' *The Guardian* 28/3/06.

45. 'Testing regime dumbs down learning', *Times Educational Supplement*, 24/2/06.

46. 'Are Academies really a success?', *Times Educational Supplement*, 10/3/06.

47. '£37,000 bonuses for exam success', *Bristol Metro* 17/11/05.

48. *Times Educational Supplement*, 24/2/06.

49. Richard Aldrich, *An Introduction to the History of Education*, p. 211.

50. 'Maths "dumbed down" at GCSE', *Times Educational Supplement*, 24/2/06.

51. Dylan Wiliam, 'Content then process', 2007.

52. Margaret Reid, Louise Clunies-Ross, Brian Goacher and Carol Vile, 'Mixed Ability Teaching: Problems and Possibilities', *Educational Research*, 1981, 24(1), pp. 3–10.

53. 'Government fails to achieve targets on setting', *The Independent*, 9/2/06.

54. Richard Aldrich, *An Introduction to the History of Education*, p. 37.

55. Guy Claxton, *An Intelligent Look at Emotional Intelligence*, Association of Teachers and Lecturers: London, 2005.

56. Peter Rogers, A. Kainth and H. Smit, 'A drink of water can improve or impair mental performance depending on small differences in thirst', *Appetite*, 2001, 36, pp. 57–8. Heinz Valtin, ' "Drink at least eight glasses of water a day." Really?' *American Journal of Physiology*, 2002, 283, pp. R993–1004.

57. Deena Weinberg and colleagues, *Journal of Cognitive Neuroscience*, 2007, reviewed in *The Psychologist*, 2007, 20(8), p. 461.

58. Quoted in R. Jones, 'Smart brains: neuroscientists explain the mystery of what makes us human', *American School Board Journal*, 1995, 182(11), pp. 22–6.

59. See Frank Coffield, David Moseley, Elaine Hall and Kathryn Ecclestone, *Learning styles and pedagogy in post-16 learning: a systematic and critical review*, Learning and Skills Research Centre, 2004.

60. Howard Gardner, *Intelligence Reframed: Multiple Intelligence for the 21st Century*, Basic Books: New York, 2000.

61. John White, *Intelligence, Destiny and Education*, Routledge: London, 2006. See also *The Guardian* 31/5/05.

62. See George Lakoff and Mark Johnson, *Metaphors We Live By*, Chicago University Press: Chicago IL, 1981.

63. The assembly-line analogy has been well delineated by, for example, Hedley Beare, *How We Envisage Schooling in the 21st Century*, SSAT: London, 2006; Peter Senge et al., *Schools That Learn*, Nicholas Brealey: London, 2000.

64. This version of the factory metaphor is described by Hermine Marshall, 'Beyond the workplace metaphor: the classroom as a learning setting', *Theory into Practice*, 1990, 29(2), pp. 94–101.

65. Lauren Resnick, 'Making America smarter', *Education Week Century Series*, 1999, 18(40), pp. 38–40.

66. This derives from the version of an old Polish story recounted by Ram Dass in *Still Here*, Putnam: New York, 2000.

67. The old view of intelligence is described in detail in Ken Richardson, *The Making of Intelligence* (Weidenfeld and Nicholson: London, 1999), from which the Spens Report quotation is taken.

68. For a detailed examination of the inextricable intertwining of nature and nurture, see, for example, Judith Rich Harris, *No Two Alike: Human Nature and Human Individuality*, WW Norton: New York, 2006.

69. See Carol Dweck, *Mindset: The New Psychology of Success*, Random House: New York, 2007. For a detailed discussion of Dweck's recent research, see Po Bronson, 'How not to talk to your kids', in *New York Magazine*, 20/2/07.

70. Angela Duckworth and Martin Seligman, 'Self-discipline outdoes IQ in predicting academic performance of adolescents', *Psychological Science*, 2005, 16(12), pp. 939–44.

71. Lauren Resnick, 'Making America Smarter'.

72. David Perkins and Tina Grotzer, 'Teaching intelligence', *American Psychologist*, 1997, 52(10), pp. 1125–33.

73. See Carol Dweck, *Mindset: The New Psychology of Success*

74. Baumeister et al., *Psychological Science in the Public interest*, 2003, 4, pp. 1–44.

75. Melanie Phillips, *All Must Have Prizes*, Little Brown: London, 1998, p. 12.

76. Shamala Kumar and Carolyn Jagacinski, 'Imposters have goals too: the imposter phenomenon and its relationship to achievement goal theory', *Personality and Individual Differences*, 2006, 40, pp. 147–57.

77. All these results come from Carol Dweck's research.

78. Richard Dawkins, *The Selfish Gene*, Oxford University Press: Oxford, 1996; Susan Blackmore, *The Meme Machine*, Oxford University Press: Oxford, 1999.

79. Philip Tetlock, 'Accountability: a social check on the fundamental attribution error', *Social Psychology Quarterly*, 1985, 48(3), pp. 227–36.
80. 'Test chiefs reject plan to spot A-level stars at 11', *Times Educational Supplement*, 3/3/06; See also *Daily Telegraph*, 29/12/06.
81. See Guy Claxton and Sara Meadows, 'Brightening up: how children learn to be gifted', in Thomas Balchin, Barry Hymer and Dona Matthews (eds), *The Routledge Companion to Gifted Education*, Routledge: London, 2008.
82. Erica McWilliam, *How to Survive Best Practice*, University of New South Wales Press: Sydney, 2002.
83. See Pierre Hadot, *What Is Ancient Philosophy?*. Harvard University Press: Cambridge MA, 2002.
84. Werner Heisenberg, *Physics and Philosophy*, Allen and Unwin: London, 1963.
85. Christina Stathopolou and Stella Vosniadou, 'Exploring the relationship between physics-related epistemological beliefs and physics understanding', *Contemporary Educational Psychology*, 2007, 32, pp. 255–81.
86. Michael Gibbons, Camille Limoges, Helga Nowotny, Simon Schwartzman, Peter Scott and Martin Trow, *The New Production of Knowledge: The Dynamics of Science and Research in Contemporary Societies*, Sage: London, 1994.
87. See Jane Gilbert, *Catching the Knowledge Wave? The Knowledge Society and the Future of Education*, New Zealand Council for Educational Research Press: Wellington, New Zealand, 2005.
88. Terezinha Nunes, Analucia Schliemann and David Carraher, *Street Mathematics and School Mathematics*, Cambridge University Press: Cambridge, 1993.
89. See, for example, Pascal Boyer, *Religion Explained: The Human Instincts that Fashion Gods, Spirits and Ancestors*, William Heinemann: London, 2001.
90. Michael Lewis, *Next: The Future Just Happened*, WW Norton: New York, 2001.
91. Plato, *The Republic*, Dover: New York, 2000.
92. David Perkins, 'Post-primary education has little impact on informal reasoning', *Journal of Educational Psychology*, 1985, 77(5), pp. 562–71. I described the results of Perkins' study in these three different groups, as he does, because, of course, you can't compare eleven-year-olds directly with post-graduates for the simple reason that the total populations from

which each group is drawn are wildly different. If graduates think better than pre-teens, it may just be because they are a highly selected population, not because they have 'consumed' more years of education.

93. Richard Andrews, Carole Torgerson, Sue Beverton, Allison Freeman, Terry Locke, Graham Low, Alison Robinson and Die Zhu, 'The effect of grammar teaching on writing development', *British Educational Research Journal*, 2006, 32(1), pp. 39–55. Reaction by Seaton reported in *The Independent*, 19/1/05.

94. Hammond Tarry and Nicholas Emler, 'Attitudes, values and moral reasoning as predictors of delinquency', *British Journal of Developmental Psychology*, 2007, 25(2), pp. 169–83.

95. Dylan Wiliam, 'Content then process: teacher learning communities in the service of formative assessment', In D. B. Reeves (ed.), *Ahead of the curve: the power of assessment to transform teaching and learning* Solution Tree: Bloomington, IN, 2007, pp. 183–204. 97.

96. Jo Boaler, *Experiencing School Mathematics*, Open University Press: Buckingham, 1997.

97. David Hargreaves, *The Challenge of the Comprehensive School*, Routledge and Kegan Paul: London, 1982, p. 64.

98. See for example, Marcus du Sautoy, *The Music of the Primes*, HarperPerennial: London, 2004.

99. Martin Hughes, *Children and Number: Difficulties in Learning Mathematics*, Blackwell: Oxford, 1986.

100. Stephen Ceci, *On Intelligence: A Bioecological Treatise on Intellectual Development*, Harvard University Press: Cambridge, MA, 1996.

101. Jonathan Haidt, *The Happiness Hypothesis*.

102. Mihaly Csikszentmihalyi, *Finding Flow: The Psychology of Engagement with Everyday Life*, Basic Books: New York, 1998. Research on students achievement and flow reported in Daniel Goleman, *Emotional Intelligence*, Bantam: New York, 1996.

103. A recent article in the *Psychologists' Research Digest* is entitled 'We're useless at predicting how what happens will make us feel', and it reports the research to prove it.

104. Some of the ideas here are borrowed from, and/or developed in conversation with, David Perkins. His book *Whole Game Learning* is forthcoming.

105. Julia Flutter and Jean Rudduck, *Consulting Pupils: What's in it for Schools?* RoutledgeFalmer: London, 2004.

106. One of the first and best books to describe this kind of learning is Donald Hebb's *The Organization of Behavior*, Wiley: New York, 1949. A more recent exposition can be found in Manfred Spitzer, *The Mind Within the Net*, MIT Press: Cambridge MA, 1999.

107. See for example Joseph LeDoux, *The Emotional Brain*, Simon and Schuster: New York, 1998. Chris Frith, *Making Up the Mind*, Blackwell: Oxford, 2007.

108. Antonio Damasio, *Descartes' Error*, Picador: London, 1995.

109. Guy Claxton, *An Intelligent Look at Emotional Intelligence*. The Association of Teachers and Lecturers: London, 2005.

110. Dianne Berry and Donald Broadbent, 'On the relationship between task performance and associated verbalisable knowledge', *Quarterly Journal of Experimental Psychology*, 1984, 36A, pp. 209–31. Mark Coulson, 'The cognitive function of confusion', paper presented to the British Psychological Society London Conference, December 1995.

111. Guy Claxton, *Wise Up: Learning to Live the Learning Life*, Bloomsbury: London, 2000; Guy Claxton, *Hare Brain, Tortoise Mind: Why Intelligence Increases When You Think Less*, Fourth Estate: London, 1997. Ap Dijksterhuis, 'Think different: the merits of unconscious thought in preference development and decision making', *Journal of Personality and Social Psychology*, 2004, 87(5), pp. 586–98.

112. Bruce Mangan, 'Taking phenomenology seriously: the "fringe" and its implications for cognitive research', *Consciousness and Cognition*, 1993, 2, pp. 89–108.

113. The amplifier of selective attention is discussed more fully in Andy Clark, *Being There: Putting Brain, Body and World Together Again*, MIT Press: Cambridge MA, 1997. These amplifiers are also more fully discussed in my book Guy Claxton, *Live and Learn: The Psychology of Growth and Change in Everyday Life*, Harper and Row: London, 1984.

114. Sara Meadows, *The Child as Thinker*, Routledge: London, 2006.

115. Andy Clark and Annette Karmiloff-Smith, The cognizer's innards: a psychological and philosophical perspective on the development of thought, *Mind and Language*, 1993, 8(4), pp. 487–519.

116. Susan Hurley and Nick Chater (eds), *Perspectives on Imitation: From Neuroscience to Social Science*, MIT Press: Cambridge MA, 2005.

117. Michael Tomasello, *The Cultural Origins of Human Cognition*, Harvard University Press: Cambridge MA, 1999.

118. Elkhonon Goldberg, *The Executive Brain*, Oxford University Press: New York, 2001.

119. This theory is elaborated by Colin Martindale, 'Biological bases of creativity', In Robert Sternberg (ed.), *Handbook of Creativity*, Cambridge University Press: Cambridge, 1999.

120. See Guy Claxton, 'Creative glide space', In Chris Bannerman, Joshua Sofaer and Jane Watt (eds) *Navigating the Unknown*, Middlesex University Press: London, 2006.

122 James Dillon, *The Practice of Questioning*, Routledge: London, 1990. Thanks to Lawrence Smith for drawing this research to my attention.

122. Albert Einstein, *Ideas and Opinions*, Souvenir Press: London, 1986.

123. Mary Belenky, Blythe Clinchy, Nancy Goldberg and Jill Tarule, *Women's Ways of Knowing: The Development of Self, Voice and Mind* (Basic Books: New York, 1988) charts such changes in a group of adult women going back to university study.

124. Chris Woodhead, *Class Wars*, Little Brown: London, 2002.

125. See for example, Sir Anthony Hopkins' techniques, as told to Gaby Wood, 'A dark and stormy knight', *The Guardian*, 5/12/1998.

126. In America, the phrase 'character education' can refer to a movement that tries to develop in young people a particular set of moral characteristics – honesty, restraint, 'clean-living', 'good behaviour' and so on. My use of the phrase is rather different.

127. Chris Woodhead, *Class Wars*, p. 57.

128. Richard Sennett, *Respect: The Formation of Character in an Age of Inequality*, Penguin: London, 2003. Neil Postman, *Technopoly: The Surrender of Culture to Technology*, Alfred A. Knopf: New York, 1992.

129. James Lovelock, *The Revenge of Gaia*, Allen Lane: London, 2006.

130. Warwick Mansell, *Education by Numbers: The Tyranny of Testing*, Politico's Publishing: London, 2007.

131. Errolyn Wallen, 'Nelson's victory', in Chris Bannerman, Joshua Sofaer and Jane Watt (eds), *Navigating the Unknown: The Creative Process in Contemporary Performing Arts*, Middlesex University Press: London, 2006.

132. Art Costa and Bena Kallick, *Discovering and Exploring Habits of Mind*, Association for Supervision and Curriculum Development: Alexandria, VA, 2000. David Perkins, Eileen Jay and Shari Tishman, 'New conceptions of thinking: from ontology to education',

Educational Psychologist, 1993, 28(1), pp. 67–85. Ron Ritchhart, *Intellectual Character: What It Is, Why It Matters and how to Get It,* Jossey-Bass: San Francisco, 2002.

133. W. Harlen and R. Deakin-Crick, 'A systematic review of the impact of summative assessment and tests on students' motivation for learning', *Research Evidence in Education Library.* EPPI-Centre, Social Science Research Unit: London, 2002.

134. Paul Black, Claire Harrison, Christine Lee, Bethan Marshall and Dylan Wiliam, *Assessment for Learning: Putting it into Practice,* Open University Press: Buckingham, 2003.

135. Allan Shoenfeld, 'Learning to think mathematically: problem-solving, metacognition, and sense-making in mathematics', in Douglas Grouws (ed.), *Handbook of Research on Mathematics Teaching and Learning,* Information Age Publishing: New York, 2006.

136. See Karen Vaughan, *Changing Lanes: Young People Making Sense of Pathways,* New Zealand Council for Educational Research, August 2003.

137. Jo Boaler, *Experiencing School Mathematics,* Open University Press: Buckingham, 1997.

138. Quoted in the Industrial Society report, 1997.

139. The ASPIRE project is funded by NESTA and directed by professor Anna Craft of Exeter university. See *http://schome.open.ac.uk/ wikiworks/index.php/Aspire_Pilot_Provocations.*

140. Marshall McLuhan, Quentin Fiore and Jerome Agel, *The Medium is the Message,* Gingko Press: Corte Madera CA, 2001

141. Peter Collett, *Book of Tells,* Bantam: London, 2004.

142. Kevin Dunbar, 'How scientists really reason: scientific reasoning in real-world laboratories', in Robert Sternberg and Janet Davidson (eds), *The Nature of Insight,* MIT Press: Cambridge MA, 1996.

143. This idea derives from the work of New Zealand early childhood expert Margaret Carr. See her book *Assessment in Early Childhood Settings: Learning Stories,* Paul Chapman: London, 2001.

144. Roger Osborne and Peter Freiberg, *Learning in Science,* Heinemann: Auckland, 1985.

145. Jo Boaler, *Experiencing School Mathematics.*

146. WALT and TIB were developed by Shirley Clarke. See her book *Formative Assessment in Action: Weaving the Elements Together,* Hodder Murray: London, 2005.

147. Guy Claxton, Louise Edwards and Vicki Scale-Constantinou, 'Cultivating creative mentalities', *Thinking Skills and Creativity*, 2006, vol. 1, pp. 57–61

148. I've drawn here on an article by Ray Tarleton, 'Create new measures of success', *Times Educational Supplement*, 14/01/2005.

149. Eileen Carnell and Caroline Lodge, *Supporting Effective Learning*, Paul Chapman: London, 2002.

150. Ellen Langer, *The Power of Mindful Learning*, Da Capo Press: Cambridge MA, 1997.

151. Ellen Langer, *The Power of Mindful Learning*.

152. The many ingenious innovations at Villiers High School are described in their book: Juliet Strang, Philip Masterson and Oliver Button, *ASK: How to Teach Learning to Learn in the Secondary School*, Crown House: Carmarthen, Wales, 2006.

153. Chris Watkins, 'Learning about learning enhances performance', *Research Matters No. 13*, National School Improvement Network: London, 2001.

154. Sally Wellbourn, 'Giving learning a hand', in Julie Fisher, Guy Claxton and Alison Price (eds), *Playing for Life: The Oxfordshire/Guy Claxton Project*, Oxfordshire County Council, 2006.

155. Mary James et al., *Learning How to Learn*, Routledge: London, 2006.

156. Patricia Smiley and Carol Dweck, 'Individual differences in achievement goals among young children', *Child Development*, 1994, 65, pp. 1723–43. Margaret Carr, *Assessment in Early Childhood Settings: Learning Stories*, Paul Chapman: London, 2000.

157. Kurt Vonnegut, *Mother Night*, Vintage: New York, 1992.

158. Anne McCrary Sullivan, 'Notes from a marine biologist's daughter: on the art and science of attention', *Harvard Educational Review*, 2000, 70(2), pp. 211–28.

159. Cardiff Schools Service, *Learning to Learn: Enquiries into Building Resourceful, Resilient and Reflective Learners*, Cardiff Schools Service Publications, 2005.

160. See Jerome Kagan, *Galen's Prophecy: Temperament in Human Nature*, Basic Books: New York, 1994.

161. Mark Lepper and David Greene, *The Hidden Costs of Reward*, Lawrence Erlbaum: Mahwah NJ, 1988.

162. Po Bronson, 'How not to talk to your kids', *New York Magazine*, 20/02/2007.

163. Pamela Frome and Jacquelynne Eccles, 'Parents' influence on children's achievement-related perceptions', 1998, *Journal of Personality and Social Psychology*, 74, pp. 435–52.

164. Doreen Arcus, cited in Kagan, *Galen's Prophecy: Temperament in Human Nature.* ·

165. Shawn Green and Daphne Bavelier, 'Effect of action video games on the spatial distribution of visuospatial attention', *Journal of Experimental Psychology: Human Perception and Performance*, 2006, 32(6), pp. 1465–78.

166. See *http://ofstednews.ofsted.gov.uk/article/238*.

167. James Delingpole, *The Independent on Sunday*, 2/12/07.

168. Geoff Mulgan, *Good and Bad Power: The Ideals and Betrayals of Government*, 2007, Allen Lane, London. Quoted in David Hargreaves' pamphlet *System Re-Design – 1*, SSAT: London, 2007.

169. Ian Mitchell, 'A perspective on teaching and learning', in John Baird and Jeff Northfield (eds), *Learning from the PEEL Experience*, Monash University Press: Melbourne Australia, 1992.

170. Hannah Green and Celia Hannon, *Their Space*, Demos: London, 2007.

171. Jonathan Haidt, *The Happiness Hypothesis*, William Heinemann: London, 2006. Richard Layard, *Happiness: Lessons from a New Science*, Allen Lane: London, 2005. Richard Layard, 'Happiness and the teaching of values', *CentrePiece*, Summer 2007, pp. 18–23.

Index